"Understandest thou, what thou Readest?"

A Pictorial Guide of Bible Secrets

By

Nathanyel Ben Israel

For Maccabee Productions LLC

Order this book online at www.trafford.com
or email orders@trafford.com

Most Trafford titles are also available at major online book retailers.

Print information available on the last page.

ISBN: 978-1-4120-8051-4 (sc)

Trafford rev. 10/03/2018

www.trafford.com
North America & international
toll-free: 1 888 232 4444 (USA & Canada)
fax: 812 355 4082

All praises to Yah the Father and Yah the Son for calling me into the Truth.
Dedicated to my beautiful children, **Gaba, Sysy,** and **Neme**, and my wife **Shamarah**, my help meet
and pillar of rest. **Barak Shar** continue to be stong and diligent, **Ahrayal**, never let anyone quench
your spirit, see you've provoked a good work. **Kanigabar** stay faithful, hold fast to what you
have and **Paryah** stand firm, you have so much to offer. I pray this inspires the dead of our
people to wake up, love one another and go into the vineyard and labor. *Until then, Messiah
comes, regardless of mans enmity.*
Maranatha.
www.israelunite.org

To The Reader

In Acts 8:30,31 a young man was reading the scriptures and the disciple Phillip asked him **"Understandest thou, what thou readest?"** the man responded "How can I except some man should **guide me?"** This book is meant solely as a guide to understanding the basic meaning of scriptures not as a substitute for the Holy Bible.

This guide book is by no means an attempt to make one bitter, neither is it meant as a personal attack against anyone. Christ said "Blessed is he, who is not offended in me ." The Apostle Paul asked in Galatians 4:16 **"Have I become your enemy because I tell you the truth?"** Discovering the truth has been my personal life's commitment, and helping others achieve **Biblical understanding** which has been kept secret in the earth for the past 400 years. You shall know the truth and the truth shall make you free. This is the way, walk ye in it!

Nathanyel Ben Israel

Table of Contents

The Holy Bible

- *Psalms 147:19:* He sheweth his word unto Jacob, his statutes and his judgments **unto Israel.**
  20: **He hath not dealt so with any nation:** and as for his judgments, they have not known them. Praise ye the LORD.

- *Romans 3:1:* What advantage then hath **the Jew**? or what profit is there of circumcision?
  2: Much every way: chiefly, because that **unto them were committed the oracles of God.**

- *Baruch 3:35:* This is our God, and there shall none other be accounted of in comparison of him
  36: He hath found out all the way of knowledge, and hath **given it unto Jacob his servant, and to Israel his beloved.**

- *According to the Old and New Testaments and the Apocrypha, **the Bible was given to the Israelites only**, not all nations.*

THE LETTER "J"

- The letter "J" was created in the 1700's.

- The King James (Iames) version Bible of 1611 had no "J" in it's text and **included** the 14 books of the Apocrypha.

- King James versions today have actually been revised since 1769 and **do not** include the Apocrypha.

THE TRUE NAME

- Today's common name Jehovah, was derived from **YHWH** and retained a 3 syllable sound. **YHWH,** pronounced **Ya-Ha-WaH,** became **JHVH,** pronounced Je-Ho-VaH.
- Jesus has several variations based upon Matthew 1:21 and Acts 7:45 in the Hebrew text. Yahawashi/ Yahshua/ Yashua
- **Psalms 68:4** "….by his name JAH" which is properly **"YAH,"** which is the shortened form of **YHWH.**
- The prefix **YAH,** is found in both: The heavenly Fathers name and his Son's name.
- **YAH** the Father and **YAH** the Son.

King Iames 1611

- There was no "J" in this translation, The letter "J" was created in the 1700's.

- King James **gathered 47 scholars** and divided them into 6 groups. Three groups translated the 39 books of the Old testament. One group for the 14 books of the Apocrypha and 2 groups for the 27 books of the New testament. This gives us a total of 80 books.

The Apocrypha

- The original King James Bible version 1611 contained the sixty-six books we have today, as well as the books in the Apocrypha. The Apocrypha explains the history between the Old and New Testaments. The Old Testament ends with Israel under the Persian captivity in "Malachi" and the New Testament begins with Rome dominating Israel and seemingly the world in "Matthew". There is a lot of missing history that was bridged by the Apocrypha books. It explains how and why the Persians gave the Israelites their freedom, some returning to their homeland, some remaining and some sailing to another land. The apocrypha also explains the rise of the Greek empire prophesied by Daniel as well as the reign of the pagan Roman empire.

- Note: The word Apocrypha means "secret" or "hidden" books.

- The Apocrypha contains:
  The secret to understanding Genesis chapter 1 (which is the history of the creation)
  II Esdras chapter 6.
  The history on how a remnant of the Ten Tribes of Israel, migrated to the Americas: II Esdras 13:40-45, proving the Puerto Ricans, Dominicans, Native Americans, Panamanians etc. are Israelites.
  The missing parts of Esther, and her private prayer before approaching the Persian king and the dream of Mordechi.
  What the three Hebrew children sang while in the fiery furnace.

- The prophet Daniel as a youth being filled with the holy spirit.

- The repentant prayer of king Manasses while in prison.

- The history of the Greek Empire (which is the beginning of the Edomites' [Caucasian] ruler ship of the earth, starting with Alexander): I Maccabees 1:1-7.

  The Hellenistic period, when Jews were forced to convert to the customs and language of the Greeks to become gentiles or face death: I Maccabees 1:41-64.

I Maccabees 3:48

- "And laid open the book of the law, wherein the heathen had sought to <u>paint the likeness of their images.</u>"

- Today many Greek and Russian orthodox clergy are hired iconoclasts. <u>Their job is to white wash all the black art remaining of the Israelites</u> throughout Europe since the Dark ages.

I Maccabees 3:48

- "And laid open the book of the law, wherein the heathen had sought to <u>paint the likeness of their images."</u>

- Leonardo DaVinci used the Borgias family as his models & Michelangelo was hired to paint these renaissance images throughout Europe.

Cesare Borgia was the model for the new image of Christ

2 Corinthians 11:4 " For if he that cometh preacheth **another Jesus**, whom we have not Preached, or if ye receive another spirit, which ye have not received, or another gospel, which ye have not accepted, ye might well bear with him."

For more details see pages 84-88.

The Real Christ

- Revelation 1:14: His head and **his hairs were white like wool**, as white as snow; and his eyes were as a flame of fire;
  15: And his **feet like unto fine brass, as if they burned in a furnace;** and his voice as the sound of many waters.

- Daniel 10:6: His body also was like the beryl, and his face as the appearance of lightning, and his eyes as lamps of fire, and **his arms and his feet like in color to polished brass,** and the voice of his words like the voice of a multitude.

- Both scriptures prove Christ is a Black man with white wooly hair.

Color in the Bible

- Lamentations 5:10 Our skin was **black** like an oven because of the terrible famine.

- Job 30:30 My skin is **black upon me, and my** bones are burned with heat.

- Acts 13:1 Now there were in the church that was at Antioch certain prophets and teachers; as Barnabas, and Simeon that was called **Niger**, and Lucius of Cyrene, and Manaen, which had been brought up with Herod the tetrarch, and Saul.

- Acts 21:37: And as Paul was to be led into the castle, he said unto the chief captain, May I speak unto thee? Who said, Canst thou speak Greek?
  38: **Art not thou that Egyptian**, which before these days madest an uproar, and leddest out into the wilderness four thousand men that were murderers?
  39: But Paul said, I am a man which am a **Jew** of Tarsus, a city in Cilicia, a citizen of no mean city: and, I beseech thee, suffer me to speak unto the people.

The Israelite Prophets portrayed black on Church of the Voronet, painted at the end of the 15 century in Eastern Europe.

12

Color in the Bible

- **Song of Solomon 1:5 I am black**, but comely, O ye daughters of Jerusalem, as the tents of Kedar, as the curtains of Solomon.

- **Daniel 10:6** His body also was like the beryl, and his face as the appearance of lightning, and his eyes as lamps of fire, and **his arms and his feet like in colour to polished brass**, and the voice of his words like the voice of a multitude.

- **Jeremiah 8:21** For the hurt of the daughter of my people am I hurt; **I am black**; astonishment hath taken hold on me.

- **Lamentations 4:8** Their visage is **blacker than a coal**; they are not known in the streets:

Adam & Eve

- **Genesis 2:7**: And the LORD God formed man of **the dust of the ground,** and breathed into his nostrils the breath of life; and man became a living soul. Genesis 2:22: And the rib, which the LORD God had taken from man, made he a woman, and brought her unto the man.

- This is one of a thousand black skinned paintings located in Eastern Europe. Church of the Voronet painted in the 1400's.

Isaiah 36:1

- "Now it came to pass in the fourteenth year of king Hezekiah, that Sennacherib king of Assyria came up against all the defenced cities of Judah, and took them."

- Stone relief from ancient ruins of Nineveh dated 701 B.C. Look at the coarse corn row hair texture on these Negroid Israelite captives.

Exodus 3:9

- " Now therefore, behold, the cry of the children of Israel is come unto me: and I have also seen the oppression wherewith the Egyptians oppress them."

- These Israelite women are portrayed mourning the loss of a nobleman. Notice these Negroid women's dark brown complexion and coarse textured hair.

- Taken from a wall painting of a high Egyptian Official at Thebes, during the reign of the Pharaoh Amenhotep the 4th during the 18th Dynasty.

Exodus 12:40

- "Now the sojourning of the children of Israel, who dwelt in Egypt, was four hundred and thirty years."

- These Israelites are portrayed taking part in a funeral procession crossing the Nile river. Examine their brown complexions and kinky hair.

- From the tomb of Neferhotep at the end of the 18th dynasty.

Exodus 1:13

- *13:* "And the Egyptians made the children of Israel to serve with rigor:
  14: And they made their lives bitter with hard bondage, in morter, and in brick, and in all manner of service in the field: all their service, wherein they made them serve, was with rigor."
- The Israelites are portrayed black skinned in all the Egyptian tombs which they served.
- Below is a wall painting from the tomb of Rechmire, governor during the reign of Pharaoh Thutmose the 3rd in the 18th dynasty.

Pharaohs

- Exodus 1:8 "Now there arose up a **new King** over Egypt, which knew not Joseph" This new kingdom of rulers cared nothing for the fame of Joseph and how he saved Egypt.

- The Israelites served slavery in ancient Egypt from the 17th dynasty, through the entire 18th dynasty and beginning of the 19th dynasties.

- A few famous Egyptians that had the Israelites as slaves are Queen Nefertiti, Pharaohs; Hatshepsut, Thutmose the 3rd , Ramses the 2nd, and Amenhotep the 3rd .

Joseph

- **Psalms 105:17** He sent a man before them, even **Joseph,** who was sold for a servant:

  18: Whose feet they hurt with fetters: he was laid in iron:

  19: Until the time that his word came: the word of the LORD tried him.

  20: The king sent and loosed him; even the ruler of the people, and let him go free.

  21: He made him lord of his house, and ruler of all his substance:

  22: To bind his princes at his pleasure; <u>and teach his senators wisdom.</u>

  23: Israel also came into **Egypt;** and Jacob **sojourned in the land of Ham.**

•Joseph taught the Egyptians wisdom and Africa was called the land of Ham.

20

Moses

- Acts 7:22 And <u>Moses was learned in all the wisdom of the Egyptians</u>, and was mighty in words and in deeds. *23:* And when he was full forty years old, it came into his heart to visit his brethren the children of Israel.

- Hebrews 11:24: By faith Moses, when he was come to years, <u>refused to be called the son of Pharaoh's daughter;</u> *25:* Choosing rather to suffer affliction with the people of God, than to enjoy the pleasures of sin for a season;

- Moses learned all Egyptian science and their god systems, but repented and refused to be known as an African prince.

The Apostle Paul

- **Acts 21:37**: And as Paul was to be led into the castle, he said unto the chief captain, May I speak unto thee? Who said, Canst thou speak Greek?
  38: Art not **thou that Egyptian,** which before these days madest an uproar, and leddest out into the wilderness four thousand men that were murderers?
  39: But Paul said, **I am a man which am a Jew** of Tarsus, a city in Cilicia, a citizen of no mean city: and, I beseech thee, suffer me to speak unto the people.
- **The Apostle Paul looked like an Egyptian/African.**

Jet Black image of Egyptian King Tutankhamen 18th Dynasty.

How to Read the Bible

- **Isaiah 28:*10:*** For precept must be upon precept, precept upon precept; line upon line, line upon line; here a little, and there a little: Meaning a precept or line from one chapter must be used to explain another precept or line from another chapter and likewise a precept or line from the Old testament must be used to explain another precept or line in the New Testament.

- **John 5:*39:*** Search the scriptures; for in them ye think ye have eternal life: and they are they which testify of me.

- ***Acts 17:11:*** These were more noble than those in Thessalonica, in that they received the word with all readiness of mind, and searched the scriptures daily, whether those things were so.

- Searching the scriptures means precept upon precept line upon line. Remember for proper understanding of the New Testament you must understand the Old Testament because the New Testament letters are based upon the Old Testament scriptures.

Isaiah 29:11,12

- *11:* And the vision of all is become unto you as the **words of a book that is sealed**, which men deliver to one that is learned, saying, Read this, I pray thee: and he saith, I cannot; for it is sealed:

- The vision of all you see in the world is recorded in the Bible but it's sealed to so called learned ministers having theology doctorates.

- *12:* And the book is delivered to him that is not learned, saying, Read this, I pray thee: and he saith, I am not learned.

- Even the self taught minister who mimics the so called learned minister cannot reveal the Bible truths or secrets.

The Truth Behind Slavery

Daniel 12:4 "But thou, O Daniel, shut up the words, and seal the book, even to the time of the end: many shall run to and fro, and knowledge shall be increased."

This proves the true understanding of the BIBLE would be **sealed**/unknown, until **the time of the end which is today**: many of our people **run to and fro man made religions**, and **knowledge of science has been increased** i.e. space travel, computers, cell phones etc.

•Who are the Blacks really? And why did they go into slavery as a nation?

Deuteronomy 28:15

- " But it shall come to pass, **if thou wilt not hearken** unto the voice of the LORD thy God, to observe **to do all his commandments** and his statutes which I command thee this day; that **all these curses shall come upon thee,** and overtake thee:"

- Let's examine the curses that came upon the Israelites.

Deuteronomy 28:16

- "Cursed shalt thou be in the city, and <u>cursed shalt thou be in the field.</u>"

- Blacks were cursed in every city that they lived in and were cursed to pick fields of cotton, sugar cane etc.

Deuteronomy 29:17

- "Cursed shall be thy basket and thy store."
- Our savings and businesses do poorly as a whole.

Deuteronomy 28:29

- " And thou shalt grope at noonday, as the blind gropeth in darkness, and thou shalt not prosper in thy ways: and thou shalt be only <u>oppressed</u> and **spoiled evermore**, and <u>**no man shall save thee.**</u>"

- Many great Black leaders tried to save us from oppression, but all have failed.

Deuteronomy 28:23

- "And thy heaven that is **over thy head shall be brass**, and the earth that is under thee shall be **iron**."
- The slaves had brass bells over their head and iron shackles on their ankles.

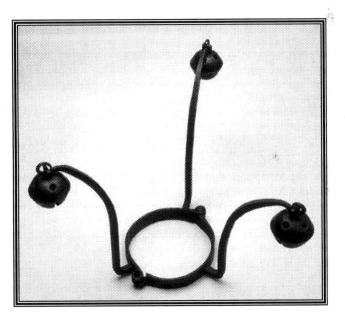

<u>Deuteronomy 28:32</u>

- "Thy sons and thy
  daughters shall be given
  unto another people,
  and thine eyes shall
  look, and fail with
  longing for them all the
  day long: and there
  shall be no might in
  thine hand."

Deuteronomy 28:37

- "And thou shalt become an astonishment, a **proverb, and a byword,** among all nations whither the LORD shall lead thee."

- A proverb, and a byword means to be renamed and labeled outside of your Biblical name. These are **gentile names**; such as niggers, negroes, colored, Blacks, Afro Americans, African Americans, Jamaicans, Haitians, Brazilians etc.

Israelites also became known as Gentiles, for more detail see pages 45-50

Deuteronomy 28:41

- "Thou shalt beget sons and daughters, but thou shalt not enjoy them; for they shall go into captivity."

Deuteronomy 28:48

- "Therefore shalt thou serve thine enemies which the LORD shall send against thee, in hunger, and in thirst, and in nakedness, and in want of all things: and he shall put a <u>yoke of iron upon thy neck,</u> until he have destroyed thee."

Deuteronomy 28:61

- "Also <u>every sickness,</u> <u>and every plague,</u> which is not written in the book of this law, them will the LORD bring upon thee, until thou be destroyed."

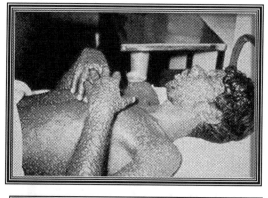

Deuteronomy 28:65,66

- *65:* And **among these nations shalt thou find no ease,** neither shall the sole of thy foot have rest: but the LORD shall give thee there a trembling heart, and failing of eyes, and **sorrow of mind:**

  66: And **thy life shall hang in doubt before thee;** and thou shalt fear day and night, **and shalt have none assurance of thy life:**

36

Deuteronomy 28:68

- "And the LORD shall bring thee into Egypt again with <u>ships,</u> by the way whereof I spake unto thee, Thou shalt see it no more again: and there **ye shall be sold** unto your enemies **for bondmen and bondwomen**, and no man shall buy you."

- The curses Moses prophesied, fit the Blacks that went into slavery on ships. **This proves they are the children of Israel.**

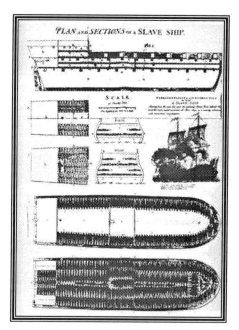

Spiritual Egypt

- Exodus 20:2 "I am the Lord thy God, which have brought thee out of the land of **Egypt, out of the house of Bondage.**"

- Egypt is synonymous for Bondage/slavery. So the Israelites went into bondage again by "Ships" and were sold to their enemies.

- The same hard bondage that we suffered in ancient **Egypt,** we suffer in **America.**

- **Notice the similar yokes of iron.**

- The above chained captives are shown on painted clay plaques from Egypt in a structure erected by the Pharaoh, Ramses the 2nd from the 19th dynasty.

So what about CHRIST?

- *LUKE 1:68:* Blessed be the Lord God of Israel; for he hath visited and redeemed his people,
  69: And hath raised up an horn of salvation for us in the house of his servant David;
  70: As he spake by the mouth of his holy prophets, which have been since the world began:
  71: **That we should be <u>saved from our enemies</u>, and from the hand of all that hate us;**
  72: To perform the mercy promised to our fathers, and to remember his holy covenant;

- Christ must return and save the Israelites from their enemies; that's according to the mercy promised and the holy covenant.

Why don't the descendants of Black slaves know who they are?

- Why don't the nations acknowledge them?

- Why don't they speak Hebrew?

- Why don't they know their true heritage?

- Why was their nationality as **Israelites** changed?

Psalms 106:35,36

- *35:* But were mingled among the heathen, and **learned their works.** *36:* And they **served their idols**: which were a snare unto them.

- We **learned** how to foolishly <u>act like</u> we received a spirit from God.

- The slaves mimicked screaming, shouting, dancing in the isles and muttering in made up tongues from the slave masters. **This is not the Holy Spirit.**

- And we **served** the slave masters images of God and Christ.

Deuteronomy 32:26

- "I said, I would **scatter them** into corners, I would make the **remembrance of them to cease** from among men:"

- We were forced into ghettoes and slums throughout the world, our true identity as Israelites has been forgotten.

Psalms 83:1-4

- *1:* Keep not thou silence, O God: hold not thy peace, and be not still, O God.
2: For, lo, thine enemies make a tumult: and they that hate thee have lifted up the head.
3: **They have taken crafty counsel against thy people, and consulted against thy hidden ones.**
4: They have said, Come, and let us cut them off from being a nation; *that the name of Israel may be no more in remembrance.*

- The United Nations have taken crafty counsel against the true Biblical Israelites. The Religions, Politics, and School Systems of the world have craftily been set up to deceive us. Our nationality as Israel is no longer in our remembrance.

Jeremiah 17:4

- _"And thou, even thyself, shalt discontinue from thine heritage that I gave thee;_ and _I will cause thee to serve thine enemies in the land which thou knowest not:_ for ye have kindled a fire in mine anger, which shall burn for ever."

- We have **discontinued from our heritage as Israelites,** no longer keeping Gods laws and holidays but became comfortable as Negroes and Blacks keeping false pagan holidays as Christians or Muslims etc.

- We were forced to serve the British, French and Spanish nations in America, the Caribbean and other lands we knew not.

We became Gentiles

- *Romans 9:24:* Even us, whom he hath called, not of the **Jews** only, but also **of the Gentiles**? *25:* As he saith also in Osee, I will call them my people, which were not my people; and her beloved, which was not beloved.
26: And it shall come to pass, that in the place where it was said unto them, **Ye are not my people; there shall they be called the children of the living God.**

- *Hosea 1:10:* Yet the number of the children of Israel shall be as the sand of the sea, which cannot be measured nor numbered; and it shall come to pass, that **in the place where it was said unto them, Ye are not my people, there it shall be said unto them, Ye are the sons of the living God.**
11: Then shall the **children of Judah and the children of Israel be gathered together,** and appoint themselves one head (CHRIST), and they shall come up out of the land —(the rapture) : for great shall be the day of Jezreel.

- *Proving the Jews and Gentiles Paul spoke of, are really the two kingdoms of Judah and scattered Israel.*

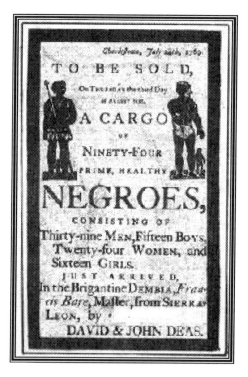

I Maccabees 1:41-58

- *The Greeks attempted to **force the Israelites** to follow their customs and religions.*
- *41:* Moreover king Antiochus wrote to his whole kingdom, that all should be one people,
  42: And every one should leave his laws: so all the heathen agreed according to the commandment of the king.
  43: **Yea, many also of the Israelites consented to his religion, and sacrificed unto idols, and profaned the Sabbath.**
  44: For the king had sent letters by messengers unto Jerusalem and the cities of Juda that they should follow the strange laws of the land,
  45: And forbid burnt offerings, and sacrifice, and drink offerings, in the temple; and that they should profane the Sabbaths and festival days:
  46: And pollute the sanctuary and holy people:
  47: Set up altars, and groves, and chapels of idols, and sacrifice swine's flesh, and unclean beasts:
  48: That they should also leave their children uncircumcised, and make their souls abominable with all manner of uncleanness and profanation:
  49: **To the end they might forget the law, and change all the ordinances.**
  50: <u>And whosoever would not do according to the commandment of the king, he said, he should die.</u>

- *51:* In the selfsame manner wrote he to his whole kingdom, and appointed overseers over all the people, commanding the cities of Juda to sacrifice, city by city.
52: Then many of the people were gathered unto them, to wit every one that forsook the law; and so they committed evils in the land;
53: And drove the Israelites into secret places, even wheresoever they could flee for succour.
54: Now the fifteenth day of the month Casleu, in the hundred forty and fifth year, they set up the abomination of desolation upon the altar, and builded idol altars throughout the cities of Juda on every side;
55: And burnt incense at the doors of their houses, and in the streets.
- *56:* And when they had rent in pieces the books of the law which they found, they burnt them with fire.
57: And whosoever was found with any the book of the testament, or if any committed to the law, the king's commandment was, that they should put him to death.
58: Thus did they by their authority unto the Israelites every month, to as many as were found in the cities.

2 Maccabees 6:1-9

- *Here is another excerpt from the Apocrypha which bridges the gap between Malachi during the reign of the Persians and Matthew during the Roman domination. This proves how rebellious Israelites became gentiles.*

- *1:* Not long after this the king sent an old man of Athens to compel the Jews to depart from the laws of their fathers, and not to live after the laws of God:
2: And to pollute also the temple in Jerusalem, and to call it the temple of Jupiter Olympius; and that in Garizim, of Jupiter the Defender of strangers, as they did desire that dwelt in the place.
3: The coming in of this mischief was sore and grievous to the people:
4: For the temple was filled with riot and revelling by the Gentiles, who dallied with harlots, and had to do with women within the circuit of the holy places, and besides that brought in things that were not lawful.
5: The altar also was filled with profane things, which the law forbiddeth.
6: Neither was it lawful for a man to keep sabbath days or ancient fasts, **or to profess himself at all to be a Jew.**

- *7:* And in the day of the king's birth every month they were brought by bitter constraint to eat of the sacrifices; and when the fast of Bacchus was kept, the Jews were compelled to go in procession to Bacchus, carrying ivy.

  8: Moreover there went out a decree to the neighbour cities of the heathen, by the suggestion of Ptolemee, against the Jews, that they should observe the same fashions, and be partakers of their sacrifices:

  9: And whoso would not <u>**conform themselves to the manners of the Gentiles**</u> should be put to death.

- Proving the Israelites were forced to become Gentiles which explains why Paul was an Apostle to the Gentiles in Romans 11:13, Acts 13:46 and Galatians 2:8,9 etc.

Greek speaking Jews

- Bronze statue of Greek speaking Jew with dred locks dated about 200B.C.

- Often called 'Hellenists', **these Israelites had conformed to the customs of the Greeks**. Some however returned to the Levitical covenant, some did not and some repented in Christ..

- John 12:20: And there were certain **Greeks** among them that came up to worship at the feast: *21:* The same came therefore to Philip, which was of Bethsaida of Galilee, and desired him, saying, Sir, we would see Jesus.

- Acts 16:1: Then came he to Derbe and Lystra: and, behold, a certain disciple was there, named Timotheus, the son of a certain woman, which was a Jewess, and believed; but his father was a **Greek:**

- Romans 10:12: For there is no difference between the Jew and **the Greek:** for the same Lord over all is rich unto all that call upon him.

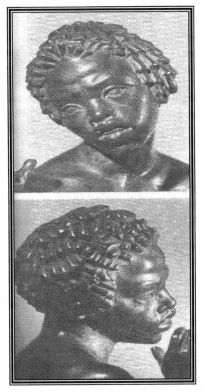

Our Language

According to prophecy, it is not necessary for Israelites to learn or speak Hebrew today.

• **Isaiah 28:11** "For with stammering lips and another tongue will he speak to this people."

• **1st Corinthians 14:19**: "Yet in the church I had rather speak five words with my understanding, that by my voice I might teach others also, than ten thousand words in an unknown tongue."

• **Zephaniah 3:8**: "Therefore wait ye upon me, saith the LORD, until the day that I rise up to the prey: for my determination is to gather the nations, that I may assemble the kingdoms, to pour upon them mine indignation, even all my fierce anger: for all the earth shall be devoured with the fire of my jealousy.
9: **For then will I turn to the people a pure language**, that they may all call upon the name of the LORD, to serve him with one consent."

• So after the final world war the Lord promises to give the Israelites the pure Hebrew language. This Proves the Hebrew dialects spoken today are corrupt.

Making Judah and Israel One

- *Ephesians 2:14:* For he is our peace, who **hath made** <u>both one</u>, and hath broken down the middle wall of partition between us;

  15: Having abolished in his flesh the enmity, even the law of commandments contained in ordinances (sacrifices); **for to make in himself of** <u>twain one new man</u>, so making peace;

Based on-

Ezekiel 37:21: And say unto them, Thus saith the Lord GOD; Behold, I will take the children of Israel from among the heathen, whither they be gone, and will gather them on every side, and bring them into their own land:

22: And <u>**I will make them one nation**</u> in the land upon the mountains of Israel; and one king shall be king to them all: <u>**and they shall be no more two nations, neither shall they be divided into two kingdoms any more at all:**</u>

52

Grafting in Israel and Judah

- *Jeremiah 11:16:* The LORD called thy name, **A green olive tree, fair, and of goodly fruit:** with the noise of a great tumult he hath kindled fire upon it, and **the branches of it are broken.**
  17: For the LORD of hosts, that planted thee, hath pronounced evil against thee, for the evil of **the house of Israel and of the house of Judah,** which they have done against themselves to provoke me to anger in offering incense unto Baal.

- *Isaiah 5:4* What could have been done more to my vineyard, that I have not done in it? wherefore, when I looked that it should bring forth grapes, brought it forth **wild grapes**?

- According to scriptural precepts when Israelites willingly disobeyed the Law they became the wild branches.

- *Romans 11:17:* And if **some of the branches be broken off,** and thou, being a wild olive tree, **wert graffed in** among them, and with them partakest of the root and fatness of the olive tree;

Grafted In

- *Ezekiel 37:19:* Say unto them, Thus saith the Lord GOD; Behold, I will take the stick of Joseph, which is in the hand of **Ephraim, and the tribes of Israel his fellows,** and will put them with him, even with the stick of **Judah,** and **make them one stick, and they shall be one in mine hand.**

- The two sticks are Israel and Judah; prophesied to be grafted together in YHWH's hand.

- *Romans 11:24:* For if thou wert cut out of the olive tree which is wild by nature, and wert graffed contrary to nature into a good olive tree: how much more shall these, which be the natural branches, be graffed into their own olive tree?

The letters of the Apostle Paul are all based on The Old Testament prophesies.

ROMANS 9:1-31

1: I say the truth in Christ, I lie not, my conscience also bearing me witness in the Holy Ghost,

2: That I have great heaviness and continual sorrow in my heart.

3: For I could wish that myself were accursed from Christ for my brethren, my   kinsmen according to the flesh:

4: Who are Israelites; to whom pertaineth the adoption, and the glory, and the covenants, and the giving of the law, and the service of God, and the promises;

So contrary to Christianity, the adoption (Christ dying on the cross) the glory (the Kingdom of heaven), the covenants (old testament and new testament), and the law, and the service (Lev.25:55) and all the promises in the Bible belong only to the Israelites.

5: Whose are the fathers, and of whom as concerning the flesh Christ came, who is over all, God blessed for ever. Amen.

Whose are the fathers of the Holy Scriptures (the Israelites) and as concerning the flesh (nationality) Christ came and died for the Israelites as per the promises!

6: Not as though the word of God hath taken none effect. For they are not all Israel, which are of Israel:

They are not all Israel which are of Israel because some of them ie. Scribes and Pharisees reject Christ. That's why in John 8:44 Christ told those rebellious Israelites 'you are of your father the devil'.

55

7: Neither, because they are the seed of Abraham, are they all children: but, In Isaac shall thy seed be called.

Neither because they are descendants of Abraham, are they Children of God. But the promise is through Abraham's son Isaac.

8: That is, they which are the children of the flesh, these are not the children of God: but the children of the promise are counted for the seed.

According to John 1:13 the flesh refers to the will of "man". So the children of the flesh are the nations that came from Hagar's son Ishmael (Genesis 25:12-16) and Keturah's children (Genesis 25:1-4).

9: For this is the word of promise, At this time will I come, and Sara shall have a son.

Paul is explaining the promise came thru Sarah's son Isaac.

10: And not only this; but when Rebecca also had conceived by one, even by our father Isaac; *the promise then came thru one son of Rebecca.*

11: (For the children being not yet born, neither having done any good or evil, that the purpose of God according to election might stand, not of works, but of him that calleth;)

Rebecca had fraternal twins, and God chose one son and rejected the other before they did either good or bad so it was according to Gods election, not deeds.

12: It was said unto her, The elder shall serve the younger.

God foretold that the elder son Esau would serve the younger son Jacob.

- *13:* As it is written, Jacob have I loved, but Esau have I hated.

So God loves Jacob/Israel and hates Esau/Edom, contrary to Christian doctrine.

14: What shall we say then? Is there unrighteousness with God? God forbid.

Is God wicked for hating Esau/Edom? No. (also read Malachi 1:1-4)

15: For he saith to Moses, I will have mercy on whom I will have mercy, and I will have compassion on whom I will have compassion.

The Lord told Moses he has mercy and compassion on whomever he chooses. Mankind has nothing to say!

16: So then it is not of him that willeth, nor of him that runneth, but of God that sheweth mercy.

Proving no one can will himself to be the people of God, nor can you run to evangelize and build churches to make yourself the people of God.

17: For the scripture saith unto Pharaoh, Even for this same purpose have I raised thee up, that I might shew my power in thee, and that my name might be declared throughout all the earth. *So the Lord raised Egypt up to be the greatest kingdom on earth so that HE could show his awesome power by destroying the might of Egypt!*

18: Therefore hath he mercy on whom he will have mercy, and whom he will he hardeneth.

The Lord had mercy upon the Israelites but hardened Pharoahs heart, all for His divine purpose.

19: Thou wilt say then unto me, Why doth he yet find fault? For who hath resisted his will?

Why does the Lord find fault with people if everyone does according to His will?

20: Nay but, O man, who art thou that repliest against God? Shall the thing formed say to him that formed it, Why hast thou made me thus?

No one can question the Lord. Can a pot question the potter that made him?

21: Hath not the potter power over the clay, of the same lump to make one vessel unto honour, and another unto dishonour?

Just as a Potter has power over clay to make one lump into a vessel to drink from and of the same lump make another vessel to defecate in. The Creator has that same power over man.

22: What if God, willing to shew his wrath, and to make his power known, endured with much longsuffering the vessels of wrath fitted to destruction:

So in this time, what if the Lord wants to show his anger again, and to make his great power known in the earth again, endured with much patience the vessels of wrath (Esau/Edom) created for destruction (Isaiah 34:5)

23: And that he might make known the riches of his glory on the vessels of mercy, which he had afore prepared unto glory,

And that the Lord might reveal the riches of his glory on the vessels of mercy; the Israelites, who are captive under Edom, the vessels of wrath just as they were captive under Egypt.

24: Even us, whom he hath called, not of the Jews only, but also of the Gentiles?

Even us the Lord called, not of Judah only, but also of the tribes of Israel?

25: As he saith also in Osee, I will call them my people, which were not my people; and her beloved, which was not beloved.

26: And it shall come to pass, that in the place where it was said unto them, Ye are not my people; there shall they be called the children of the living God.

The scattered tribes of Israel were called outcasts by the Israelites that returned to keep the law. Paul is quoting Hosea 1:10,11 proving the gentiles here are the Israelites.

Let's examine the entire quote in Hosea 1:10: Yet the number of the children of Israel shall be as the sand of the sea, which cannot be measured nor numbered; and it shall come to pass, that in the place where it was said unto them, Ye are not my people, there it shall be said unto them, Ye are the sons of the living God.

11: Then shall the children of Judah and the children of Israel be gathered together, and appoint themselves one head, and they shall come up out of the land: for great shall be the day of Jezreel.

Back to Romans 9:27 "Esaias also crieth concerning Israel, Though the number of the children of Israel be as the sand of the sea, a remnant shall be saved:"

Again Paul proves according to Isaiah 10:20-22 he is still referring to Israel, that as numerous as they are among all nations there is a remnant that shall be saved in Christ.

28: For he will finish the work, and cut it short in righteousness: because a short work will the Lord make upon the earth.

29: And as Esaias said before, Except the Lord of Sabaoth had left us a seed, we had been as Sodoma, and been made like unto Gomorrha. *Except the Lord of Hosts had left Israel a seed (Christ) we would all be destroyed as Sodom and Gomorrha.*

30: What shall we say then? That the Gentiles, which followed not after righteousness, have attained to righteousness, even the righteousness which is of faith.

Meaning the scattered Israelites (outcasts) which followed __NOT__ after the Old Covenant of Levi with the sacrifices, have attained to righteousness, indeed the righteousness of faith; which is faith in Christ which includes keeping the commandments.

31: But Israel, which followed after the law of righteousness, hath not attained to the law of righteousness.

But Israel which followed after the Old covenant of Levi, have not attained to the law of righteousness because they did not have faith in Christ, ie. The New Covenant.

32: Wherefore? Because they sought it not by faith, but as it were by the works of the law. For they stumbled at that stumblingstone;

Why? Because those Israelites didn't seek righteousness by faith in Christ but by doing the Old Covenant laws like animal sacrifice etc. through the Levites.

33: As it is written, Behold, I lay in Sion a stumblingstone and rock of offence: and whosoever believeth on him shall not be ashamed.

So many Israelites that only believed in the Old Covenant of Levi stumbled at Christ as the Savior; and whosoever of that remnant of Israel (outcasts/scattered) which believe in Christ shall not be ashamed.

SHALOM

60

Is Africa The Motherland?

- *Galatians 4:26:* But Jerusalem which is above is free, which is the mother of us all.

- How come many of our people came out of Africa?

Matthew 2:13

- *13:* "And when they were departed, behold, the angel of the Lord appeareth to Joseph in a dream, saying, Arise, and take the young child and his mother, and **flee into Egypt,** and be thou there until I bring thee word: for Herod will seek the young child to destroy him."

- So Joseph hid the young Christ in Egypt, which is in <u>North East Africa.</u> Proving Christ and his parents were Black people.

- For more about Herod see pages 79 & 80.

Luke 21:20,21

- *20:* And when ye shall see Jerusalem compassed with armies, then know that the desolation thereof is nigh. *21:* Then let them which are in Judaea **flee to the mountains**; and let them which are in the midst of it **depart out**; and **let not them that are in the countries enter thereinto.**

- Many Israelites fled into the mountains of **Africa**. Remember, Joseph took his wife Mary and their son Christ and fled into **Africa** fleeing persecution based on Matthew 2:13.

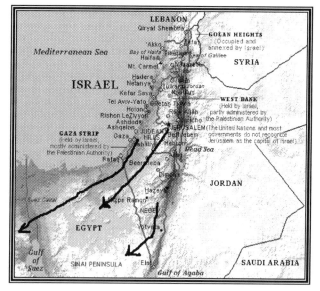

Luke 21:24

- "And they shall fall by the edge of the sword, and <u>shall be led away</u> **captive into all nations**: and

- _<u>Jerusalem shall be trodden down of the **Gentiles**,</u>_ until the times of the Gentiles be fulfilled."

- Christ is teaching us that the true Israelites would be led away as slaves into all nations and the Gentiles/heathen nations would live in Jerusalem.

64

Joel 3:2

- "I will also gather all nations, and will bring them down into the valley of Jehoshaphat, and will plead with them there for my people and for my heritage Israel, **whom they have scattered among the nations**, and *__parted my land__*."

- YHWH God promises to gather all nations for war because the true Israelites have been **scattered among the nations as slaves and the land of Israel has been parted/divided** by Caucasian Israeli's (see pg.73) and Arab Palestinians.

65

Joel 3:3

- "And they have **cast lots for my people**; and have given a <u>boy for an harlot</u>, and sold a girl for wine, that **they might drink.**"

- Our <u>boys were forced to become breeders</u>, and our girls were sold for wine so that they (slave masters) **might party sexually.**

Joel 3:4,5

- *4:* Yea, and what have ye to do with me, O **Tyre, and Zidon** (**Africans**), and all the coasts of **Palestine** (**Arabs**)? will ye render me a recompense? and if ye recompense me, swiftly and speedily will I return your recompense upon your own head;
5: Because ye have taken my silver and my gold, and have carried into your temples my goodly pleasant things:

- The Slave trade involved the **Africans** and the **Arabs** selling the **Israelites**. They also robbed the Israelite temples.

Joel 3:6

- "The children also of Judah and the children of Jerusalem have ye sold unto the Grecians, that ye might remove them <u>far from their border.</u>"

- Proves **Israelites** were sold to the Greeks/Caucasians, **Not Africans.**

Fort Judah: the holding cell of the slaves.

Isaiah 22:17,18

- *17:* "Behold, the LORD will **carry thee away with a mighty captivity**, and will surely cover thee.
  18: He will surely violently turn and **toss thee like a ball into a large country:** there shalt thou die,...."

- We were carried away with a mighty captivity and tossed like a ball across the ocean on ships into a large country, the Americas. Read Deuteronomy 28:68.

Genesis 12:3

- *3:* And I will bless them that bless thee, and **curse him that curseth thee**: and in thee shall all families of the earth be blessed.

- **Obadiah verse 15**: For the day of the LORD is near upon all the heathen: **as thou hast done, it shall be done unto thee**: thy reward shall return upon thine own head.

Revelation 13:9,10

- 9: If any man have an ear, let him hear.

- 10: "He that leadeth into captivity shall go into captivity: he that killeth with the sword must be killed with the sword. Here is the patience and faith of the saints."

- Christ explains that any nation that leads the Israelites into slavery shall go into slavery: any nation that kills the Israelites with the sword must be killed with the sword.

Israelite slave, early 1700's

Who's really in Israel?

- If Black people are the true Biblical Israelites, then who are the Jew-ish Caucasian's living in the land of Israel ???

Ezekiel 36:5

- "Therefore thus saith the Lord GOD; Surely in the fire of my jealousy have I spoken against the residue of the heathen, and against all **Idumea (Edom)**, which have _appointed my land into their possession with the joy of all their heart, with despiteful minds_, to cast it out for a prey."

- Israel was declared a state in 1948. This was orchestrated by America, the European governments and the U.N.

Genesis 25:25

- "And the first came out <u>red all over</u> like a hairy garment; and they called his name **Esau**."

- **Verse 30** "And **Esau** said to Jacob, feed me I pray thee, with that <u>same red pottage</u>: for I am faint :therefore was his name called <u>**EDOM**</u>."

- This is the beginning of all Caucasians, they vary in red complexions. The blood shows through their skin.

Obadiah 1:1,4

- 1: The vision of Obadiah. Thus saith the Lord GOD concerning Edom;….
  4:"Though thou <u>exalt thyself as the eagle,</u> and though thou <u>set thy nest among the stars</u>, thence will I bring thee down, saith the LORD."

- The symbol of America is the eagle and in 1969 they landed on the moon proclaiming, "The Eagle has Landed!"

WHO ARE THE EDOMITES?

- Genesis 25:25: And the first came out red, all over like an hairy garment; and they called his name Esau. 26:And after that came his brother out and his hand took hold on Esau's heel; and his name was called Jacob." *Esau's color –RED is mentioned in this chapter because it was much different from his parents Isaac and Rebekah and his brother Jacob, because they were all brown skinned according to Genesis 2:7 "and the Lord God formed man of the dust of the ground,…" The dust of the ground ranges from dark brown to light brown.*

- Genesis 25:30 "And Esau said to Jacob, Feed me, I pray thee, with that same red pottage; for I am faint: therefore was his name called Edom." *Esau's complexion is red, and the blood shows through his skin, he is very hairy. He desired the red pottage and his name was called Edom which means red.*

- .Genesis 27:38: And Esau said unto his father, Hast thou but one blessing, my father? Bless me, even me also, O my father. And Esau lifted up his voice, and wept.39: And Isaac his father answered and said unto him, Behold, thy dwelling shall be the fatness of the earth, and of the dew of heaven from above; 40: And by thy sword shalt thou live, and shalt serve thy brother; and it shall come to pass when thou shalt have the dominion, that thou shalt break his yoke from off thy neck." *Esau's blessing was to dwell throughout the Earth. This was accomplished by living by the sword meaning war. Esau conquered all the brown nation's beginning with Alexander and the Greeks, followed by The Roman Empire, Great Britain and the United States of America. Edom only served Israel for a short time and after King Solomon, Edom broke loose from Israel. Read 2 Kings 8:20-22.*

- Deuteronomy 28: 49: The LORD shall bring a nation against thee from far, from the end of the earth, as swift as the eagle flieth; a nation whose tongue thou shalt not understand; 50: A nation of fierce countenance, which shall not regard the person of the old, nor shew favour to the young:" *Moses prophesied the Greeks and Romans would destroy the Israelites as the Eagle. The symbol of Greece was the Eagle as well as Rome.*

- Ezekiel 36:5 "Therefore thus saith the Lord GOD; Surely in the fire of my jealousy have I spoken against the residue of the heathen, and against all Idumea[EDOM], which have appointed my land into their possession with the joy of all their heart, with despiteful minds, to cast it out for a prey." *Edom appointed the land of Israel as theirs under the approval of the United Nations in 1948 when it was declared a state.*

- Obadiah verse 1: The vision of Obadiah. Thus saith the Lord GOD concerning Edom; We have heard a rumour from the LORD, and an ambassador is sent among the heathen, Arise ye, and let us rise up against her in battle. 2: Behold, I have made thee small among the heathen: thou art greatly despised 3: The pride of thine heart hath deceived thee, thou that dwellest in the clefts of the rock, whose habitation is high; that saith in his heart, Who shall bring me down to the ground? 4: Though thou exalt thyself as the eagle, and though thou set thy nest among the stars, thence will I bring thee down, saith the LORD."

- *Edom is despised by the dark nations and filled with much pride. At one point Edom dwelt in Mount Seir and another time in the Caucus Mountains of Georgia Russia. This is why they call themselves Caucasians.*

- *The blessing Isaac gave Esau was to conquer everyone by the sword and dwell where ever they desired throughout the earth. This resulted in great Pride causing them to ask 'WHO CAN BRING US DOWN? MEANING WHO CAN CONQUER US? because we conquered all nations!*

- *From the Greek empire to the Roman Empire, to Spain, Germany, Great Britain and America; Edom's symbol has always been the EAGLE. THEY SET THEIR NEST AMONG THE STARS AND SAID 'THE EAGLE HAS LANDED' IN 1969 WHEN THEY LANDED ON THE MOON.*

- Obadiah verse 21: "And saviors shall come up on mount Zion to judge the mount of Esau; and the kingdom shall be the Lord's." *The SAVIORS are the 144,000 recorded in Revelation 7. They shall judge/testify against Esau; and Christ shall come and set up the Kingdom. This Proves that ESAU IS THE LAST OF THE NATIONS RULING.*

- 2 Esdras 6:8 "And he said unto me, From Abraham unto Isaac, when Jacob and Esau were born of him, Jacob's hand held first the heel of Esau. 9: For <u>Esau is the end of the world, and Jacob is the beginning of it that followeth.</u>"

SHALOM

History of the Jew-ish people

- Remember all Caucasians descend from Esau, they are all Edomites. The suffix 'ish' means somewhat or close to in origin. So the word Jew-ish means somewhat of a Jew or close to in origin but not the original, as in a convert.
  Historically nations have converted to the laws and customs of the Jews (Israelites), an example of this was during the reign of Queen Esther during the Persian Empire in **Esther 8:17.**

- The Israelite John Hycranus of the tribe of Levi (**I Maccabees 13:53**) was the son of Simon, the last surviving brother of Judas Maccabeus, who was the high priest and ethnarch (*a ruler of a province or people*) of Judea from 143-34 BC. Simon made John commander of the Judean armed forces. He became high priest and ruler in succession to his father. By military and political successes John was able to expand the territory of Judea, and to strengthen its autonomy.

- **"Harpers Bible Dictionary"** page 414 under "Hycranus"and **"The complete works of Josephus"** page 279 records "*Hycranus took also Dora and Marissa, cities of Idumeans (Edomites/Caucasians) and permitted them to stay in that country, if they would <u>circumcise their genitals, and make use of the laws of the Jews</u>; and they were so desirous of living in the country of their forefathers, that they submitted to the use of circumcision, and the rest of the Jewish ways of living; at which time therefore this befell them, that they were hereafter no other than <u>Jews.</u>*"

- This gives us a better understanding of King Herod and King Agrippa the 2nd. They were Jewish converts. In Luke 1:5 Herod the Great was actually an Idumean (Edomite) but was called "King of Judea (Judah)" In Acts 26:3 Herods great grandson, King Agrippa, was expert in all customs and questions among the Jews. Herods family were agents of the Roman Empire because they were the same race of people. **"Harpers Bible Dictionary"** **page 385** under "Herod" says "…. *The Idumean's had been forcibly converted to Judaism by John Hycranus, and thus the family of Herod was, at least technically, <u>Jewish</u>.*"

SHALOM

Revelation 3:9

- "Behold, I will make them of <u>the synagogue of Satan, which say they are Jews, and are not, but do lie;</u> behold, I will make them to come and worship before thy feet, and to know that I have loved thee."

- Read also Revelation 2:9.

The Shield/Star of David

- **Amos 5:26** "But ye have borne the tabernacle of your Moloch and Chi'un your images, **the <u>star</u> of your god**, which ye made to yourselves."

- This symbol was never given to King David, there is **no scriptural proof.** This star has *six* points, forms *six* equilateral triangles, and in its interior forms a *six* sided hexagon.

- *6* points, *6* triangles, and the *6* sides of the hexagram. Found in idolatry & the Kabala; Jewish witchcraft.

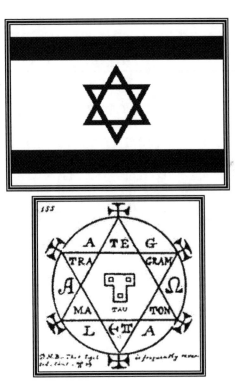

Revelation 13:13

- "And he doeth great wonders, so that he maketh <u>fire come down from heaven</u> on the earth in the sight of men,"

- Fire came down from heaven in 1945 when the atom bomb was first dropped on Hiroshima.

Revelation 13:15

- *15:* And he had power to give life unto the **image of the beast**, that the image of the beast should both speak, and cause that as <u>many as would not worship the image of the beast should be killed.</u>

- Europeans gave the **image of Cesare Borgia; the life of Christ** and as many as would not worship this image was killed.

Revelation 13:9-18

- **Verse 9**: If any man have an ear, let him hear.
  10: He that leadeth into captivity shall go into captivity: he that killeth with the sword must be killed with the sword. Here is the patience and the faith of the saints.

- *Who led the nation of Israel into captivity and killed with the sword meaning conquered by war? Remember the blessing Isaac gave Esau? Genesis 27:39 And Isaac his father answered and said unto him, Behold, thy dwelling shall be the fatness of the earth, and of the dew of heaven from above; 40:* <u>**And by thy sword shalt thou live,**</u>"

- *So Esau rules and dwells throughout the earth because he conquered all the dark nations by the sword (war). He mainly conquered the Israelites leading them into captivity and killed many by the sword. The Saints are the elect of Israel according to Psalms 50:5-7, Psalms 148:14 and we are to be patient for the Lord's judgment.*

- *The seven headed beast of Rev. 13:1-10. has the characteristics of the ancient Empires of Daniel 7:3-8. But this is the same seven headed red dragon of Revelation 12:3 which symbolizes the nation of Edom (red) because she led many into captivity and killed with the sword.,*

- *Rev.13:11:* And I beheld another beast coming up out of the earth; and he had two horns like a lamb, and he spake as a dragon *(this beast is the United States of America).*

- *having two horns like a lamb which is Christianity and Democracy; these two horns are like a lambs because they sound peaceful, righteous for all mankind, and he spake as a dragon because those two doctrines are contrary to God's laws and the testimony of Israel.*

85

- *For example: in the name of <u>Christianity</u> America slaughtered 70 million Native American Indians, stole their land and forced them onto concentration camps called reservations as well as killing over 100 million so called negroes and enslaved them, - that's the true Holocaust.*

- *Under <u>democracy</u> the Constitution allows everyone freedom of religion, if you want to worship idols you can, if you want to worship the devil you can. Behind all this and more what is proclaimed ?"GOD BLESS AMERICA & IN GOD WE TRUST".*

- *12:* And he exerciseth all the power of the first beast before him, and causeth the earth and them which dwell therein to worship the first beast, whose deadly wound was healed.

- *America exercises all the military strength of the first beast before him which was the Roman Empire and causes the earth meaning all nations (within this great melting pot) to worship/honor Pagan Rome. The days of the week and the planets, are based on Roman gods. All of the idols throughout America are based on Roman design including the statue of liberty. Rome's deadly wound was that she fell, but was healed in the forming of America.*

- *13:* And he doeth great wonders, so that he maketh fire come down from heaven on the earth in the sight of men,

- *The great wonder of fire which America made come down from heaven/the sky was the dropping of the atom bomb on Hiroshima and Nagasaki in 1945.*
  14: And deceiveth them that dwell on the earth by the means of those miracles which he had power to do in the sight of the beast; saying to them that dwell on the earth, that they should make an image to the beast, which had the wound by a sword, and did live.

- *This miracle of fire from heaven deceived all nations that dwell on the earth which he had power to do in the sight of his fellow Edomites (the beast Revelation 13:1);saying to the nations that they should accept the image of Edom Which had a wound/fell by a sword/war: ROME and did live/revived as America.*

  15: And he had power to give life unto the image of the beast, that the image of the beast should both speak, and cause that as many as would not worship the image of the beast should be killed.

- *America had power to give life to their image. The image was Cesare Borgia, the son of Pope Alexander the 6th of ROME. The life given to this image was the life of Christ, the image of the beast(Cesare Borgia, an Edomite) speaks the words of Christ. For example if you ask anyone in the world who said "I am the way the truth and the life?" they will point to the image of Cesare Borgia and proudly say "Jesus Christ". When America was young she caused many that refused to accept their image of Christ (Cesar Borgia)to be killed.*

- *16:* And he causeth all, both small and great, rich and poor, free and bond, to receive a mark in their right hand, or in their foreheads:

- *America causes all nations, small and great nations, rich and poor nations, free and bond (third world nations) to receive a mark (Democracy/Christianity) in their right hand because they physically fight and give their lives for America's doctrine or in their foreheads because they sincerely believe in America's doctrine.*

- *17:* And that no man might buy or sell, save he that had the mark, or the name of the beast, or **the number of his name**.

- *And that no nations of man might buy or sell, meaning an embargo and sanctions are imposed on any nation, which is a measure taken by America to force nations to comply with their decisions. Except he that had the mark (doctrines of democracy/Christianity),*

- *18:* Here is wisdom. Let him that hath understanding count **the number of the beast**: for it is **the number of a man**; and his number is Six hundred threescore and six.

- The number of his name is 6, the number of the beast is 6 and the number of this man is 6: 666 has no numeric formula but simply represents Edom, in particularly, America.

  SHALOM

Isaiah 14:12

- "How art thou fallen from heaven, O **Lucifer, son of the morning!** how art thou cut down to the ground, which didst weaken the nations!"

- *Lucifer means light bearer. What does the torch symbolize in the hand of the statue of Liberty? Light; This idol symbolizes that **America is the light bearer to the world.** America will be cut down to the ground because she weakened the nations by: politics, religions and war.*

Isaiah 14:13,14

- "For thou hast said in thine heart, <u>I will ascend into heaven, I will exalt my throne above the stars of God</u>: I will sit also upon the mount of the congregation, in the sides of the north: <u>I will ascend above the heights of the clouds</u>; I will be like the Most High."

- America <u>exalted it's throne to the moon by space travel</u> in 1969 and enslaved the Israelites in the sides of North America.

- America <u>ascended above the clouds with planes</u> in 1903.

Isaiah 14:1-16

- *Isaiah prophesies the LORD'S mercy upon the Israelites and the establishing of the Kingdom of heaven on Earth.*
- *1:* For the LORD will have mercy on Jacob, and will yet choose Israel, and set them in their own land: and the strangers shall be joined with them, and they shall cleave to the house of Jacob.

- *The Lord will bring the Israelites back to their homeland and the strangers/nations will be joined with us; cleaving unto us by keeping the Laws, statutes and commandments.*
  2: And the people shall take them, and bring them to their place: and the house of Israel shall possess them in the land of the LORD for servants and handmaids: and they shall take them captives, whose captives they were; and they shall rule over their oppressors.
- *The nations will serve the Israelites in the kingdom of heaven.*
  3: And it shall come to pass in the day that the LORD shall give thee **rest from thy sorrow, and from thy fear, and from the hard bondage wherein thou wast made to serve,**
- *Remember in Matthew 11:28 Christ said "come unto me all ye that labor and are heavy laden and I will give you rest." Proving he will give the faithful Israelites rest from bondage.*
  4: That thou shalt take up this proverb against the king of Babylon, and say, How hath the oppressor ceased! the golden city ceased!

- *Isaiah is prophesying the fall of the King of Babylon, which is America, the golden city.*

- *Babylon means confusion. This mighty country is a mixture of all different races, languages, religions, beliefs, and politics. America is the King of Confusion.*
  5: The LORD hath broken the staff of the wicked, and the sceptre of the rulers.
  6: He who smote the people in wrath with a continual stroke, he that ruled the nations in anger, is persecuted, and none hindereth. *America has ruled and dominated the children of Israel, and the other dark nations in anger continually. America's turn for persecution is now which is why terrorist activities are escalating. No one can stop it.*

- *7:* The whole earth is at rest, and is quiet: they break forth into singing.
  8: Yea, the fir trees rejoice at thee, and the cedars of Lebanon, saying, Since thou art laid down, no feller is come up against us.
  9: Hell from beneath is moved for thee to meet thee at thy coming: it stirreth up the dead for thee, even all the chief ones of the earth; it hath raised up from their thrones all the kings of the nations.

- *Hell from beneath is referring to the nations that caught hell under America,...like the Arab nations and others are rising up to take America down. They shall meet America as she comes down from glory. All nations will rise up against America as she begins to be persecuted by terrorism more and more.*

- *10:* All they shall speak and say unto thee, Art thou also become weak as we? art thou become like unto us?
  11: Thy pomp is brought down to the grave, and the noise of thy viols: the worm is spread under thee, and the worms cover thee.

- *The pride of America's heart (Obadiah verse 3) shall be brought down to the grave/death.* 12: How art thou fallen from heaven, O Lucifer, son of the morning! how art thou cut down to the ground, which didst weaken the nations!

- *Lucifer means light bearer. What does the torch symbolize in the hand of the statue of Liberty? Light, the idol of lady liberty symbolizes that America is the light bearer to the world.* America shall be cut down to the ground because America weakened all nations by politics, religions and war.
  13: For thou hast said in thine heart, I will ascend into heaven, I will exalt my throne above the stars of God: I will sit also upon the mount of the congregation, in the sides of the north:

- *America ascended in to heaven by space travel and landing on the moon in 1969: America sits upon/enslaved the Israelites in the ghettoes of North America.*
  14: I will ascend above the heights of the clouds; I will be like the most High. America desires to be like the most high –God, even attempting to create life by cloning.

- *America flew above the heights of the clouds in 1903 with the invention of the airplane.*
  15: Yet thou shalt be brought down to hell, to the sides of the pit.
  16: They that see thee shall narrowly look upon thee, and consider thee, saying, Is this the man that made the earth to tremble, that did shake kingdoms;

- *Proving that the King of Babylon is man (Edom) Lucifer is man (Edom) is America that made the earth to tremble that did shake kingdoms (by war).*
  SHALOM

Matthew 7

- *13:* Enter ye in at the strait gate: for <u>wide is the gate, and broad is the way, that leadeth to destruction</u>, and many there be which go in thereat:

- Christianity is the worlds largest religion that leads to destruction and many follow.

Matthew 24:5

- *5:* For many shall come in my name, saying, I am Christ; and shall deceive many.

- Christ means "Anointed". Many come in his name, saying **"I am Christian"** and deceive many.

The World of Israel

- *Isaiah 45:17:* But <u>Israel shall be saved in</u> the LORD with an everlasting salvation: ye shall not be ashamed nor confounded **world without end.**

- John 18:20: Jesus answered him, **I spake openly to <u>the world;</u>** I ever taught in the synagogue, and in the temple, **whither <u>the Jews</u> always resort;** and in secret have I said nothing.

John 3:16: For God so loved <u>the world</u>, that he gave his only begotten Son, that whosoever believeth in him should not perish, but have everlasting life.

•**The world** God so loved is <u>the world of Israel.</u>

Holidays & Commandments

- "For verily I say unto you, Till heaven and earth pass, one jot or one tittle **shall in no wise pass from the law**, till all be fulflled."- Matthew 5:18

- Christ said "If you love me **keep my commandments**."- John 14:15

- "He that saith, I know him and keepeth not his **commandments** is a LIAR, and the truth is not in him."- I John 2:4

Deuteronomy 6:2,7

- **2:** That thou mightest fear the LORD thy God, to keep all his statutes and his commandments, which I command thee, **thou, and thy son, and thy son's son, all the days of thy life;** and that thy days may be prolonged.
7: And thou shalt **teach them diligently unto thy children,** and shalt talk of them when thou sittest in thine house, and when thou walkest by the way, and when thou liest down, and when thou risest up.

Ephesians 6:4 is based upon this Law.

Biblical Holidays

Sabbath
Leviticus 23:3
Passover
Leviticus 23:5
Feast of Unleavened Bread
Leviticus 23:6
Day of Simon
I Maccabees 13
Feast of First Fruit
Leviticus 23:10
Memorial of Blowing of Trumpets
Leviticus 23:24 (7th New Moon)
Day of Atonement
Leviticus 23:27
Feast of Tabernacles
Leviticus 23:34
Feast of Dedication
I Maccabees 4, John 10:22
Destruction of Nicanor
2 Maccabees 15
Purim
Esther 9:26

These days are to be observed in the faith of Christ without the Levitical sacrifices, according to I Corinthians 5:8 and Tobit 2:1.

Sunday

- From the time of ancient Egypt and even ancient Babylon, the sun was worshipped as the main false god (the sun god, Ra). Idol worshippers chose a day to honor their false god and called it, "Sunday".
- After the death and resurrection of Christ, the enemies of our Lord were successful in infiltrating the true Church as the scriptures warned.
- **Matthew 24:11** *"And many false prophets shall arise, and shall deceive many.*
- **Acts 20: 29** *"For I know this, that after my departing shall grievous wolves enter in among you, not sparing the flock. **Verse 30** "Also of your own selves shall men arise, speaking perverse things, to draw away disciples after them."*
- After Paul and the other disciples died many false teachers entered into the church bringing lies/heresies. In time, these heretics taught that the Sabbath which God had given as a memorial of His creation was done away by Christ and Sunday was exalted as the Lords day. This made it much easier for idol worshippers to come into the church and increase the financial income of the church; if the Christians met on the same day that the pagan world did.
- There are only eight scriptures in the New Testament that mention the first day of the week.
- **Matthew 28:1** *"In the end of the Sabbath, as it began to dawn toward the first day of the week, came Mary Magdalene and the other Mary to see the sepulcher."*

- **Mark 16:1** *"And when the sabbath was past, Mary Magdalene, and Mary the mother of James, and Salome, had bought sweet spices, that they might come and anoint him.*
  2: *And very early in the morning the first day of the week, they came unto the sepulchre at the rising of the sun."*

- **Mark 16:9** *"Now when Jesus was risen early the first day of the week, he appeared first to Mary Magdalene, out of whom he had cast seven devils."*

- **Luke 24:1** *"Now upon the first day of the week, very early in the morning, they came unto the sepulchre, bringing the spices which they had prepared, and certain others with them."*
  John 20:1 *"The first day of the week cometh Mary Magdalene early, when it was yet dark, unto the sepulchre, and seeth the stone taken away from the sepulchre."*

- **John 20:19** *"Then the same day at evening, being the first day of the week, when the doors were shut where the disciples were assembled <u>for fear of the Jews</u>, came Jesus and stood in the midst, and saith unto them, Peace be unto you."*

- **Acts 20:7** *"And upon the first day of the week, when the disciples came together to break bread, Paul preached unto them, ready to depart on the morrow; and continued his speech until midnight.*
  8: *And there were many lights in the upper chamber, where they were gathered together."* **I Corinthians 16:1** *"Now concerning the collection for the saints, as I have given order to the churches of Galatia, even so do ye."*
  2: *Upon the first day of the week let every one of you lay by him in store, as God hath prospered him, that there be no gatherings when I come."*

- Notice the first five scriptures simply state that the Israelite women came to the sepulcher early in the morning and that Christ had already risen from the dead. Pagan church leaders teach that the followers of Christ gathered on the first day of the week because of some new law but **John 20:19** says that the Lord appeared to the disciples later in the day and that the reason they assembled on the first day of that week was "for FEAR of the Jews".
- The seventh scripture was **Acts 20:7,8**, it shows us that the disciples gathered to hear Paul preach because he was going to depart on the morrow (so called Monday). This is a farewell get together.
- The eighth and last scripture was **I Corinthians 16:1,2** which was about the believers coming together for the purpose of gathering money. Paul wanted this money already prepared when he got there to take it to the poor Israelites in Jerusalem.
- There is NO mention in either of those verses that teach us about a change of the Lord's Sabbath to Sunday.
- This is what Christ taught concerning this matter:
- **Matthew 5:17** *"Think not that I am come to destroy the law, or the prophets: I am not come to destroy, but to fulfill."*
- **Matthew 12: 8** *"For the Son of man is Lord even of the Sabbath day."*
  SHALOM

Thanksgiving

- **Exodus 20:13:** Thou shalt not kill.
  15: Thou shalt not steal.
  16: Thou shalt not bear false witness against thy neighbor.
  17: Thou shalt not covet thy neighbor's house, thou shalt not covet thy neighbor's wife, nor his manservant, nor his maidservant, nor his ox, nor his ass, nor any thing that is thy neighbor's.

- **Habakkuk 2:12** "Woe to him that buildeth a town with **blood**, and stablisheth **a city by iniquity!**"

- Many of Gods laws were broken to establish the United States of America.

- Thanksgiving celebrates the murder of 70 million native Indians (Israelites).

- America is a stolen country read **Job 24:2-10.**

- America was named after Amerigo Vespucci, read **Psalms 49:11.**

Jeremiah 10:1-4

- **1:** Hear ye the word which the LORD speaketh unto you, O house of Israel:

  2: Thus saith the LORD, **Learn not the way of the heathen,** and be not dismayed at the signs of heaven; for the heathen are dismayed at them.

  3: For the customs of the people are vain: **for one cutteth a tree out of the forest,** the work of the hands of the workman, **with the axe.**

  4: **They deck it with silver and with gold;** they fasten it with nails and with hammers, that it move not.

Christmas

- Christmas trees, holiday shopping sales, decorations in offices, homes, and storefronts. These are all signs of the approaching holiday season. Once again, it is the season for Israel to be sober and mindful of the laws, statues, and commandments of the Most High. We should be sober and mindful of the laws always, but in this season of increase pagan worship, we must avoid the so-called "**Holiday Spirit**".

- Jeremiah 10:2 "*Thus saith the Lord, learn not the way of the heathen, and be not dismayed at the signs of heaven; for the heathen are dismayed at them.*" So the Lord commands us not to learn the customs/traditions of the nation we are captive under. He further commands us not to fear the signs of Heaven like the sun the moon or the stars; because the nation that Israel was captive under made graven images of the signs of heaven to show their respect in worship. They made a large star and put it on top of the tree and little stars called ornaments all about the tree (read Deuteronomy 4:19).

- Jeremiah 10:3 "*For the customs of the people are vain: for one cutteth a tree out of the forest, the work of the hands of the workman, with the axe.*" Because the customs/holidays of the people are LIES: someone cuts a tree out of the forest, the job of a man with an axe .

- Jeremiah 10:4 "*They deck it with silver and with gold; they fasten it with nails and with hammers, that it move not.*" They decorate the tree with silver and with gold tinsel; they fasten the tree to stand up with nails using a hammer, so that it doesn't fall down.

- Today the world calls this holiday **Christmas.** God commanded the Prophet Jeremiah to warn us not to follow this day proving that it has nothing to do with Jesus Christ.
- The heathen have added that Christ was born on Christmas day to deceive disobedient Israelites. (Read Deut 7:25-26)

- **Proverbs 30:6** *"Add thou not unto his words, lest he reprove thee, and thou be found a LIAR."* Christianity is based upon pagan LIES and anyone that teaches Christ was born on Christmas day or that we should celebrate it for the kids, has now been found a liar!

  SHALOM

Acts 12:4

- " And when he had apprehended him, he put him in prison, and delivered him to four quaternions of soldiers to keep him; intending after **Easter** to bring him forth to the people."

- Easter has been celebrated by pagan idol worshippers and can be found in the Old Testament but only under it's original Canaanite spelling "Ashtaroth". Some times spelled Ashtoreth or Astarte . Later spelled "Ishtar" pronounced "Easter".

- **I Samuel 7: 3:** "*And Samuel spake unto all the house of Israel, saying, If ye do return unto the LORD with all your hearts, then put away the strange gods and* **Ashtaroth** *from among you,*"

Easter

- Easter is a day that is honored by today's Christians and claims to celebrate the resurrection of Jesus Christ. The holiday often involves a church service at sunrise, a feast , decorated eggs and stories about rabbits. According to the Bible however, this day has nothing to do with Christ.

- The modern spelling of Easter can only be found once in the Bible.

- **Acts 12: 1:** Now about that time Herod the king stretched forth his hands to vex certain of the church.
  2: And he killed James the brother of John with the sword.
  3: And because he saw it pleased the Jews, he proceeded further to take Peter also. (Then were the days of unleavened bread.)
  4: And when he had apprehended him, he put him in prison, and delivered him to four quaternions of soldiers to keep him; intending after **Easter** to bring him forth to the people."

- Easter has been celebrated by pagan idol worshippers and can be found in the Old Testament but only under it's original Canaanite spelling "Ashtaroth". Some times spelled Ashtoreth, Astarte, Ishtar, or Esther. Today, it's pronounced "Easter".

- **I Samuel 7: 3:** *And Samuel spake unto all the house of Israel, saying, If ye do return unto the LORD with all your hearts, then put away the strange gods and **Ashtaroth** from among you, and prepare your hearts unto the LORD, and serve him only: and he will deliver you out of the hand of the Philistines.*

- I Samuel 12: 10: *And they cried unto the LORD, and said, We have sinned, because we have forsaken the LORD, and have served Baalim and **Ashtaroth**: but now deliver us out of the hand of our enemies, and we will serve thee.*

- Ashtoroth (**Easter**) is both the goddess of fertility and the moon goddess. This idol is often portrayed as a standing female with open arms and numerous breasts (eggs) as symbols of fertility, and a turret crown. She became known as Diana of the Ephesians in which Paul and the Disciples of Christ instructed the Israelites of Ephesus not to worship, read Acts 19.

- The goddess of fertility with the numerous breasts later became depicted as a fertile rabbit with numerous eggs symbolizing life and resurrection. Every year, on the first Sunday after the first full moon after the spring equinox, a celebration was made. It was Ashtoroth Sunday (Easter Sunday) and was celebrated with rabbits and eggs.

- Ashtoroth Sunday was the day of life and resurrection and thus is changed into Easter Sunday the day Christ resurrected from the dead and incorporated into Christianity. Today families and churches throughout the world have been deceived into believing they honor the resurrection of Christ and color and play Easter Egg games complete with rabbits.

- We are warned in **2 Corinthians 6:17** *"Wherefore come out from among them, and be ye separate, saith the Lord, and touch not the unclean thing; and I will receive you, And will be a father unto you, and ye shall be my sons and daughters, saith the Lord Almighty."*

SHALOM

Jeremiah 44:19

- *19:* And when we burned incense to the **queen of heaven**, and poured out drink offerings unto her, did we make her cakes to worship her, and pour out drink offerings unto her, without our men?

110

Mothers day

- Every one loves their 'Mother' even the law teaches us in Exodus 20:12 "Honour thy father and thy mother: that thy days may be long upon the land which the LORD thy God giveth thee." However man has established his own day of reverence to honor 'Mothers". This is not scriptural to do but is based on Satanic; idolatrous principles. Although early Mother's Day celebrations were nothing like the observance of Mother's Day today, the true essence and origin is the same today.

- History proves that the tradition of honoring mothers dates back to ancient cultures including Greece and Rome. In both cultures, mother goddesses were worshiped during the springtime with religious festivals. The ancient Greeks paid tribute to the powerful goddess Rhea, the wife of Cronus, known as the *Mother of the Gods*. Similarly, evidence of a three-day Roman festival in Mid-March called Hilaria, to honor the Roman goddess Magna Mater, or *Great Mother*, dates back to 250 B.C. A temple on the Palatine hill in Rome was built in honor of the Great Mother, where people would come bearing gifts to offer her and cakes.

- Mother's day however goes even deeper than that. In the Holy Scriptures the Most High has recorded that the Israelites which dwelt in Egypt followed the goddess Isis or "Queen of Heaven" as she was also called. In today's society many Catholic Christians call Mary, the mother of Christ: "The Queen of Heaven."

- **Jeremiah 44:15** *"Then all the men which knew that their wives had burned incense unto other gods, and all the women that stood by, a great multitude, even all the people that dwelt in the land of Egypt, in Pathros, answered Jeremiah, saying,*

- **16:** *As for the word that thou hast spoken unto us in the name of the LORD,* **we will not hearken unto thee.**

17: *But we will certainly do whatsoever thing goeth forth out of* **our own mouth***, to burn incense unto* **the queen of heaven***, and to pour out drink offerings unto her, as we have done, we, and our fathers, our kings, and our princes, in the cities of Judah, and in the streets of Jerusalem: for then had we plenty of victuals, and were well, and saw no evil.*

18: *But since we left off to burn incense to the* **queen of heaven***, and to pour out drink offerings unto her, we have wanted all things, and have been consumed by the sword and by the famine.*

19: *And when we burned incense to* **the queen of heaven***, and poured out drink offerings unto her, did we make* **her cakes to worship her***, and pour out drink offerings unto her, without our men?*

20: *Then Jeremiah said unto all the people, to the men, and to the women, and to all the people which had given him that answer, saying,*

21: *The incense that ye burned in the cities of Judah, and in the streets of Jerusalem, ye, and your fathers, your kings, and your princes, and the people of the land, did not the LORD remember them, and came it not into his mind?*

22: *So that the LORD could no longer bear, because of the evil of your doings, and because of the abominations which ye have committed; therefore is your land a desolation, and an astonishment, and a curse, without an inhabitant, as at this day.*

SHALOM

Unclean Food

- Leviticus 11:7 "And the swine,.. he is unclean to you. 8: **Of their flesh shall ye not eat,..**

- Isaiah 66:15 "For behold, **the Lord will come with fire**, and with his chariots like a whirlwind, **to render his anger with fury,** and his rebuke with flames of fire. 16:For by fire and by his sword will the Lord plead with all flesh: **and the slain of the Lord will be many.** 17:They that sanctify themselves in the gardens behind one tree in the midst, **eating swine's flesh,....**

Unclean Food

- **Leviticus 11:10**: And all that have not fins and scales in the seas, and in the rivers, of all that move in the waters, and of any living thing which is in the waters, they shall be an abomination unto you:

  11: They shall be even an abomination unto you; <u>ye shall not eat of their flesh,</u> but ye shall have their carcases in abomination.

- So called delicacies, Shrimps, Crabs and Lobsters are not to be eaten. They don't have BOTH fins and scales.

The Dietary law

False doctrines today search for scriptures to justify breaking the dietary laws. We shall examine the texts and prove they are wrong.

Acts 10: 10: *"And he became very hungry, and would have eaten: but while they made ready, he fell into a trance,*

11: *And saw heaven opened, and a certain vessel descending unto him, as it had been a great sheet knit at the four corners, and let down to the earth:*

12: *Wherein were all manner of fourfooted beasts of the earth, and wild beasts, and creeping things, and fowls of the air.*

13: *And there came a voice to him, Rise, Peter; kill, and eat.*

14: *But Peter said, Not so, Lord; for I have never eaten any thing that is common or unclean.*

15: *And the voice spake unto him again the second time, What God hath cleansed, that call not thou common."*

The unlearned read the previous verses and believe this history means we can eat meats which the Lord had instructed all Israel not to eat. Not so, because verse 28 explains what the visions meant.

Acts 10: 28: And he said unto them, Ye know how that it is an unlawful thing for a man that is a Jew to keep company, or come unto one of another nation; but God hath shewed me that I should not call any <u>man</u> common or unclean."

Proving the sheet knit at the four corners of the earth having a certain vessel with unclean beast etc. represented Israel scattered to the four corners of the Earth.

115

Remember the New Testament is based upon the Old Testament prophecies.

Deuteronomy 4: 27": *And the LORD shall <u>**scatter you** among the nations</u>, and ye shall be left few in number among the heathen, whither the LORD shall lead you."*

Deuteronomy 28: "64": *And the LORD shall **scatter** thee among all people, from the one end of the earth even unto the other; and there thou shalt serve other gods, which neither thou nor thy fathers have known, even wood and stone."*

Deuteronomy 32: 26": *I said, I would <u>**scatter them into corners**</u>, I would make the remembrance of them to cease from among men:"*

The Israelites had been scattered among all the nations (heathens) and learned the customs of those nations.

Psalms 106: 35 ": *But were **mingled among the heathen**, and **learned** their works."*

Now let's examine 1 Timothy 4: 1: *"Now the Spirit speaketh expressly, that in the latter times some shall depart from the faith, giving heed to seducing spirits, and doctrines of devils;*
2: Speaking lies in hypocrisy; having their conscience seared with a hot iron;
*3: Forbidding to marry, and **commanding to abstain from meats**, which God hath created to be received with thanksgiving of them which believe and know the truth.*

Of them which believe and know the TRUTH, let's examine the truth

Psalms 119: 142: *"Thy righteousness is an everlasting righteousness, and <u>**thy law is the truth.**</u>"*

John 14:6 ": *Jesus saith unto him, <u>**I am the way, the truth**</u>, and **the life**: no man cometh unto the Father, but by me."*

Meaning that in Christ, the TRUTH is you also have to keep the law.

116

They forget the prophecy about Christ in **Isaiah 42: 21:** *"The LORD is well pleased for his righteousness' sake; <u>he will magnify the law</u>, and <u>make it honourable."</u>*
Back to I Timothy 4:4: *"For every creature of God is good, and nothing to be refused, if it be received with thanksgiving:*

5: *For it is sanctified by the word of God and prayer."*

Every creature of God is good but according to the law. Let's read

Romans 7:12 *"Wherefore **the law** is holy, and **the commandment** holy, and just, and <u>good</u>."*

*Every creature of God is sanctified by the word of God. The Word of God is the Holy Scriptures and Christ declares in Hebrews 10: "7": Then said I, Lo, I come (in the **volume** of the book it is written of me,) to do thy will, O God.."*

Where in the scriptures are creatures sanctified? Sanctified means 'made clean', to learn which meats were made clean you must refer to Leviticus 11 or Deuteronomy 14. This understanding coupled with prayer is how the Lord wants us to eat our meats.

SHALOM

Numbers 15:38

- "Speak unto the children of Israel, and bid them that they make them **fringes in the borders of their garments** throughout their generations, and that they put upon the fringe of the borders a ribband of blue."

- The fringes go **around** the borders of your clothes. Look at the stone relief evidence.

- This stone relief erected around 830 B.C. Shows Jehu, a king of Israel bowing to the Assyrian King Shalamaneser

Fringes

- Examine how the fringes go around the border of their garments. Examine the coarse hair texture of the corn row hair style.

- A 7th century B.C. detail of an alabaster frieze found at an Assyrian palace portrays Israelites playing music for the Assyrian monarch.

Habakkuk 2:18

- "What profiteth <u>the **graven image**</u> that the maker thereof hath graven it; the molten image, <u>and a **teacher of lies**</u>, that the maker of his work trusteth therein, to make **dumb idols**?"

- We are not to worship graven images ie. Exodus 20:4.

- The top idol they teach to be Christ is actually the infamous "Cesare Borgias".

- The lower idol they teach to be Peter is actually the roman god "Jupiter".

Covering the head

- The tradition of wearing a Yarmulke is unscriptural. Under Messiah the Israelite man is NOT to cover his head when praying or prophesying but the woman must.

- *1 Corinthians 11:4:* Every man praying or prophesying, having his head covered, dishonoureth his head.
  5: But every woman that prayeth or prophesieth with her head uncovered dishonoureth her head: for that is even all one as if she were shaven.
  6: For if the woman be not covered, let her also be shorn: but if it be a shame for a woman to be shorn or shaven, let her be covered.
  7: For a man indeed ought not to cover his head, forasmuch as he is the image and glory of God: but the woman is the glory of the man."

- Prophesying: "....for the testimony of Jesus is the spirit of prophecy"-Revelation 19:10

Leviticus 19:27

- "Ye shall not **round the corners of your heads,** neither shalt thou **mar the corners of thy beard.**"

- Today, many black men disobey this law and **shave off** scalp hair and beards for fashion.

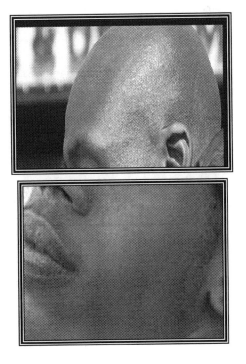

Leviticus 19:28

- "Ye shall not make any cuttings in your flesh for the dead, _nor print any marks upon you:_ I am the LORD."

- It has become fashionable to break this law- tattoos.

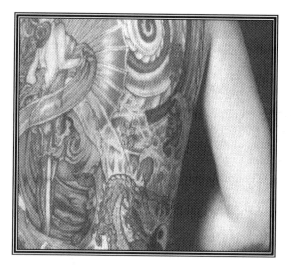

Deuteronomy 22:5

- "The <u>woman shall not wear that which pertaineth unto a man,</u> neither shall a <u>man put on a woman's garment:</u> for all that do so are abomination unto the LORD thy God."

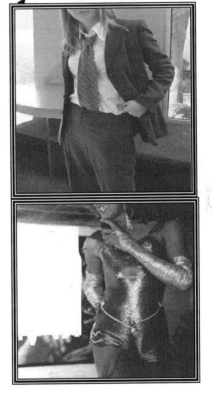

Immodest clothing

- Proverbs 7:10 "And, behold, there met him a woman with the <u>attire of an harlot</u>, and subtil of heart."

- I Timothy 2:9 "In like manner also, that <u>women</u> adorn themselves in <u>modest apparel,…</u>"

- Today, many women dress shameless.

Romans I:26,27,32

- 26: For this cause God gave them up unto vile affections: for even their **women did change the natural use into that which is against nature:** 27: And likewise **also the men,** leaving the natural use of the woman, **burned in their lust one toward another; men with men** working that which is unseemly, and receiving in themselves that recompence of their error which was meet.

- 32: Who knowing the judgment of God, that they which commit such things are worthy of death,...

Leviticus 18:18

- *18:* "Neither shalt thou take a wife to her sister, to vex her, <u>to uncover her nakedness</u>, **<u>beside the other</u>** in her life time."

- Threesome sex is fornication.

PROSPERITY

"I told da church look at yo' neighbah and say
Money 3 times. MONEY MONEY MONEY
Now grit yo' teeth.,…. And dey did! Din I got
Da holy ghost- HUM DA LOO BA BABALOO
Da money really came din!!"

Micah 3

- *11:* The heads thereof judge **for reward**, and the priests thereof teach **for hire**, and the prophets thereof divine **for money**: yet will they lean upon the LORD, and say, Is not the LORD among us? none evil can come upon us.

- Ministers today claim God is with them based on wealth.

2 Kings 5

- **26**: And he said unto him, Went not mine heart with thee, when the man turned again from his chariot to meet thee? **Is it a time to receive money,** and to receive garments, and olive yards, and vineyards, and sheep, and oxen, and menservants, and maidservants?
  27: The leprosy therefore of Naaman shall cleave unto thee, and unto thy seed for ever. And he went out from his presence a leper as white as snow.

- Gehazi, the manservant was cursed for taking money as payment to do the work of the Lord.

I Timothy 6

- *17:* Charge them that are rich in this world, that they be not highminded, nor trust in uncertain riches, but in the living God, who giveth us richly all things to enjoy;
18: <u>That they do good, that they be rich in good works, ready to distribute,</u> willing to communicate;
19: Laying up in store for themselves a good foundation against the time to come, that they may lay hold on eternal life.

Acts 2

- *42:* And they continued stedfastly in the apostles' doctrine and fellowship, and in breaking of bread, and in prayers.

  43: And fear came upon every soul: and many wonders and signs were done by the apostles.

  44: And all that believed were together, and had all things common;

  45: <u>And sold their possessions and goods, and parted them to all men, as every man had need.</u>

Women Preachers

- **I Timothy 2:12**: <u>But I suffer not a woman to teach, nor to usurp **authority over the man**, but to be in silence.</u>

- **I Corinthians 14:34**: Let your women keep silence in the churches: for it is not permitted unto them to speak; but they are commanded to be under obedience, as also saith the law.

- **Proverbs 13:13**: Whoso despiseth the word shall be destroyed: but he that feareth the commandment shall be rewarded.

Family Structure

- *The structure of the family dictates the order amongst our people. To obey God's law, promises us life but to disobey, results in single family households, broken homes, alcohol abuse, domestic violence and so on, ending in death.*

- **Titus 2:2**: That the aged men be sober, grave, temperate, sound in faith, in charity, in patience.
  3: **The aged women** likewise, that they be in behavior as becometh holiness, not false accusers, not given to much wine, teachers of good things;
  4: That they may <u>teach the young women to be sober, to love their husbands, to love their children,</u>

- (the aged women are commanded to teach young women. 2nd Timothy 1:5 and 2nd Maccabees 7:27 proves women **also taught the children**. Do all things decently and in order.)
  5: To be discreet, chaste, keepers at home, good, obedient to their own husbands, that the word of God be not blasphemed.

- *6:* Young men likewise exhort to be sober minded.
  7: In all things shewing thyself a pattern of good works: in doctrine shewing uncorruptness, gravity, sincerity,...

False Prophets

- Matthew 7:15: Beware of **false prophets**, which come to you in sheep's clothing, but inwardly they are <u>ravening wolves</u>.

- Here's how you know a false prophet:
- **Ezekiel 22:26:** Her priests have **violated my law**, and have profaned mine holy things: they have put no difference between the holy and profane, **neither have they shewed difference between the unclean and** the clean, and have **hid their eyes from my sabbaths,** and I am profaned among them.
  27: Her princes in the midst thereof are <u>like wolves ravening</u> the prey, to shed blood, and to **destroy souls, to get dishonest gain.**

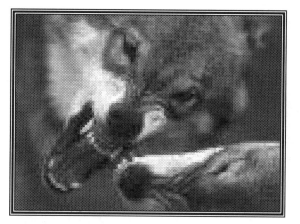

•Violate YHWH's law's
•No difference between unclean and clean food
•Reject the Sabbaths

Prophecies

- Here are a few prophecies regarding so called natural disasters; the Arab nations and America.

- Disasters will be more frequent and terrorist acts will escalate in these last days.

- All for the deliverance of Israel and the establishing of YHWH's kingdom on Earth.

Jeremiah 23

- *25:* I have heard what the prophets said, **that prophesy lies in my name,** saying, <u>I have dreamed, I have dreamed.</u>
26: How long shall this be in the heart of the prophets that **prophesy lies? yea, they are prophets of the deceit of their own heart;**
27: Which think to cause my people **to forget my name by their dreams** which they tell every man to his neighbor, as their fathers have forgotten my name for Baal.
28: The prophet that hath a dream, let him tell a dream; and **he that hath my word, let him speak my word faithfully.**

Daniel 2:42-43

- *42:* And as the toes of the feet were part of iron, and part of clay, so the kingdom shall be partly strong, and partly broken.
43: And whereas thou sawest iron mixed with miry clay, **they shall mingle themselves with the seed of men: but they shall not cleave one to another,** even as iron is not mixed with clay.

- This last kingdom is America. The Civil rights movement fulfilled this prophecy. America the great melting pot, all races mingled together, equality for all nationalities, partly strong militarily but weak by liberal and civil laws. The different races will not join together.

Daniel 7:25

- "And he shall speak great words against the most High, and shall wear out the saints of the most High, and think to change times and laws: and they shall be given into his hand until a time and times and the dividing of time."

- This last kingdom called America speaks great words against the Most High, "I'll set my nest among the stars and be like the most High." By space travel and shall wear out the saints (Israelites) in slavery through religions, politics and educational lies.

- America changes times and laws. During day light savings time, time goes back one hour in the fall or ahead one hour in the spring. They also changed The Most High's dietary laws and his holidays, i.e. the 7th day Sabbath was changed to Sunday.

- We, the Israelites have been given into Americas hand for a dispensation of time.

Isaiah 29:6

"Thou shalt be <u>visited of the LORD</u> of hosts with **thunder**, and with **earthquake**, and **great noise**, with **storm** and **tempest**, and the **flame of devouring fire.** "

The Iraqi War

- **Proverbs 21:1** The king's heart is in the hand of the LORD, as the rivers of water: he turneth it whithersoever he will.

- **Revelation 17:17** For God hath put in their hearts to fulfill his will, and to agree, and give their kingdom unto the beast, until the words of God shall be fulfilled.

- **Joel 3:2** I will also gather all nations, and will bring them down into the valley of Jehoshaphat, and will plead with them there for my people and for my heritage Israel, whom they have scattered among the nations, and parted my land.

Genesis 16:12

- **Ishmael** (father of the Arab nations)

- "And **he will be a wild man**; <u>his hand will be against every man</u>, and every mans hand against him;…."

Revelation 18:18-21

- *18:* And cried when they saw the smoke of her burning, saying, **What city is like unto this great city!**
19: And they cast dust on their heads, and cried, weeping and wailing, saying, Alas, alas, that great city, wherein were made rich all that had ships in the sea by reason of her costliness! for in one hour is she made desolate.
20: Rejoice over her, thou heaven, and ye holy apostles and prophets; for God hath avenged you on her.
21: And a mighty angel took up a stone like a great millstone, and cast it into the sea, saying, <u>**Thus with violence shall that great city Babylon be thrown down,**</u> and shall be found no more at all.

- America is the great city Babylon.

Isaiah 54:16

- *16:* Behold, I have created the smith that bloweth the coals in the fire, and that bringeth forth an instrument for his work; and **I have created the waster to destroy.**

Thermal Nuclear missile

2 Peter 3:10

- " But the day of the Lord will come as a thief in the night; in the which the heavens shall pass away with a great noise, and the elements shall melt with fervent heat, the earth also and the works that are therein shall be burned up."

Zechariah 14:12

- " And this shall be the plague wherewith the LORD will smite all the people that have fought against Jerusalem; Their flesh shall consume away while they stand upon their feet, and their eyes shall consume away in their holes, and their tongue shall consume away in their mouth."

How Do I Repent?

The way an Israelite repents is by humbling themselves to the LAWS of the Most High in Christ. This begins the process of Repenting.

The repentant Israelite must acknowledge his or her sin before the Most High thru Christ in repenting of their sins. But what is sin? According to 1ˢᵗ John 3:4: Whosoever committeth sin transgresseth also the law: **for sin is the transgression of the law.**

Proverbs 28:13 *"He that covereth his sins shall not prosper. (Meaning one that hides and continues breaking the law)* **but whoso confesseth and forsaketh them shall have mercy"**

The Israelite brother or sister that confesses their sins to the Most High and Christ must stop committing those sins and apply the commandments in the faith of Christ.

The inner man and woman must now change and humble his or herself to the scriptures as it is written. As a result of confessing your sins and departing from them, the Lord will show mercy.

Once that inner man and inner woman repents then the outward Israelite man and woman will outwardly show how an Israelite should walk according to the laws of the Most High in Christ.

Ephesians 4:23 *"And be renewed in the spirit of your mind; (Meaning Repent) what has to be cleansed from your mind is the evil it constantly entertains.*

Christ spoke of what is in our minds/ our hearts. **Mark 7:21**: *For from within, out of the heart of men, proceed evil thoughts, adulteries, fornications, murders,*

22: *Thefts, covetousness, wickedness, deceit, lasciviousness, an evil eye, blasphemy, pride, foolishness:*

23: *All these evil things come from within, and defile the man."*

Christ is explaining the wicked thoughts that come to our minds and are acted upon as well.

Verse 24 ": And that ye put on the new man, which after God is created in righteousness and true holiness"

Psalms 51:17 *" **The sacrifices of God are a broken spirit:** (Meaning That Brother or sister that has sincerely acknowledged they have sinned against the Most High will humble themselves to the commandments of the Most High)* **a broken and a contrite heart, O God, thou wilt not despise"**

The Lord will extend mercy to the Israelites that truly repent and stop committing sin such as adultery, fornication, idolatry etc. That mercy truly lies in the willingness to repent in Christ. (Read Exodus 20:6)

Psalms 19:7 *" **The law of the Lord is perfect converting the soul: the testimony of the Lord is sure"** the laws of the Most High has no faults; there is no evil in... Thou shalt not have any other gods, Thou shalt not commit adultery, Thou shalt not murder, Thou shalt not steal, Remember the Sabbath keep it holy...* **etc.** Keeping the Law Thru Christ converts the sinful mind of the Israelite man and woman.

Ephesians 4: 23 *"And be renewed in the spirit of your mind"* True repentance lies within your mind accepting the Laws of the Most High and Christ and applying them to your life everyday.

Acknowledging your sins and applying the commandments in the faith of Christ is truly being **Born again.**

Acts 3:19 *"Repent ye therefore, and be converted, that your sins may be blotted out, when the time of refreshing* (repentance and salvation thru Jesus Christ) *shall come from the presence of the Lord"*

John 3:3 *"Jesus answered and said unto him, Verily, verily, I say unto thee, except a man be born again* (keep the law in Christ)... *he cannot see the kingdom of God"*

Matthew 19: 16 *"And behold one came and said unto him, Good Master, what good thing shall I do that <u>I might inherit eternal life?</u>*

Matthew 19:17 "And he said unto him, Why callest thou me good? There is none good but one, that is God: **but if thou wilt enter into life, KEEP THE COMMANDMENTS.** SHALOM

Psalms 51:1-3, 25:7

- **Psalms 51:1** *"Have mercy upon me, O God, according to thy lovingkindness: according unto the multitude of thy tender mercies blot out my transgressions.*
  2: Wash me throughly from mine iniquity, and cleanse me from my sin.
  3: For I acknowledge my transgressions: and my sin is ever before me."

- **Psalms 25:7** *"Remember not the sins of my youth, nor my transgressions: according to thy mercy remember thou me for thy goodness' sake, O LORD."*

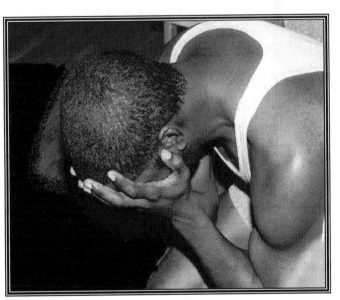

The SEAL of YHWH

- **Revelation 7:2:** And I saw another angel ascending from the east, having <u>the seal of the living God</u>: and he cried with a loud voice to the four angels, to whom it was given to hurt the earth and the sea,
  3: Saying, Hurt not the earth, neither the sea, nor the trees, <u>till we have sealed the servants of our God in their foreheads.</u>
  4: And I heard the number of them which were sealed: <u>and there were sealed an hundred and forty and four thousand of all the tribes of the children of Israel.</u>

- **Isaiah 8:16:** Bind up the testimony, <u>seal the law among my disciples.</u>

- **Revelation 14:12:** Here is the patience of the saints: <u>here are they that keep the commandments of God, and the faith of Jesus.</u>

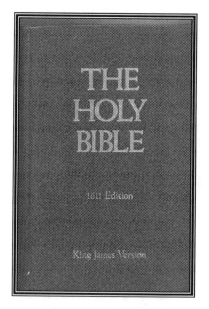

The 144,000 are the leading men Of Israel, Kings and Priests under Christ.

151

Israel is the Great Multitude

- **Revelation 7:9** After this I beheld, and, lo, **a great multitude, which no man could number, of all nations, and kindreds, and people, and tongues,** stood before the throne, and before the Lamb, clothed with white robes, and palms in their hands;

- **Hosea 1:10** Yet the number of the children of <u>Israel shall be as the sand of the sea, which cannot be measured nor numbered;</u> and it shall come to pass, that in the place where it was said unto them, Ye are not my people, there it shall be said unto them, Ye are the sons of the living God.

- **Acts 2:5** And there were dwelling at Jerusalem <u>Jews, devout men, out of every nation under heaven.</u>

Read 2nd Esdras 2:38-28 for more detail and proof.

152

The 12 Tribes of Israel

Judah

Reuben

Gad

Asher

Nepthali

Manasseh

Simeon

Levi

Issachar

Zebulon

Joseph (Ephraim)

Benjamin

1200 men of each tribe shall be leaders of the great multitude of Israelites that no man could number out of all nations according to Revelation 7:1-9,

Revelation 14:1-4, Acts 2:5, and Hosea 1:10,11.

Baptism

According to Webster's dictionary, the term Baptize is defined as: to be dipped under water; to purify; to cleanse; to sanctify as being baptized in the Spirit.

In today's world, many Israelites are under the misconception that they still have to be dunked in water to be saved. Therefore, the question must be asked, what was the true meaning behind water baptism? Should one believe that all it takes to receive salvation is a little water and saying the words, "*I believe*" *and* ignore God's laws?

John the Baptist's water baptism symbolized the spiritual death of the disobedient-sinful person being dipped and he or she rises from the water a new creature repentant-keeping God's commandments. But today all too often that same sinful person rises as a wet sinful person, nothing changes, except the frequent use of 'God bless you' and they attend church on Sundays, join the choir and celebrate false holidays.

Psalms 119:9: "*Wherewithal shall a young man cleanse his way? by taking heed thereto according to thy word.*" In order to "*cleanse*" your sinful ways and be baptized in **Christ**, repenting Israelites must take "*heed*" to the "*word*" of the **Most High** by keeping the Commandments of Christ, Read 1st John 2:3-4.

Jeremiah 2:22: "*For though thou wash thee with nitre, and take thee much sope, yet thine iniquity is marked before me, saith the Lord God.*"

The cleansing of the body with "*nitre*" or "*sope*" (soap) does not remove sin before the **Most High**. Therefore, it is the washing of the mind/spirit with the laws of **Christ** that will remove "*iniquity*."

    Jeremiah 4:14 "*O Jerusalem, wash thine heart from wickedness, that thou mayest be saved. How long shall thy vain thoughts lodge within thee?*"

Jeremiah told Israel to wash their heart (mind) from wickedness! Only the law can wash the heart. What's in the heart?

Christ explains what's in our heart (the mind),...

Mark 7:21 "*For from within, out of the heart of men, proceed evil thoughts, adulteries, fornications, murders,*

Verse **22** "*Thefts, covetousness, wickedness, deceit, lasciviousness, an evil eye,*

blasphemy, pride, foolishness:

verse **23** "*All these evil things come from within, and defile the man.*"

Isaiah 1:16 "*Wash you, make you clean; put away the evil of your doings from before mine eyes; cease to do evil;*"

So even Isaiah explains the Wash that makes us clean is putting away our evil doings. How? Keep the Law!

I Peter 3:21: "*The like figure whereunto even baptism doth also now save us (not the putting away of the filth of the flesh, but the answer of a good conscience toward **God**,) by the resurrection of Jesus Christ.*"

N*ot the putting away of the filth of the flesh*," meaning by sprinkling or dipping the body in water (water baptism). Therefore, the only baptism that can "*save us*" is a "*good conscience toward God,*" which means the Israelites must keep the Commandments in **Christ** (spiritual baptism).

Ephesians 5:26: "*That he might sanctify and cleanse it with the washing of water by the word,*" The **Most High** will cleanses us from sin by the "law" which is in **Christ**, read John 1:1-4,14.

Again, only when an Israelite repents and keeps the Laws of **Christ**, will the Lord "*sanctify*" and "*cleanse*" them, and not by the dipping in water. This can also be proved in Psalms 19 and 1st Corinthians 10.

Psalms 19:7: "*The law of the Lord is perfect, converting the soul: the testimony of the Lord is sure, making wise the simple.*" The keeping of the "*law*" through Christ is the wisdom that converts the soul from sin. This is truly being born again/baptized.

1st Corinthians 10:1-4: "*Moreover, brethren, I would not that ye should be ignorant, how that all our fathers were under the cloud, and all passed through the sea;*

Verse 2, *And were all __baptized unto Moses__ in the cloud and in the sea;*

Verse 3, *And did all eat the same spiritual meat;*

Verse 4, *And did all drink the same spiritual drink: for they drank of that spiritual Rock that followed them: and that Rock was Christ."*

*"And were all **baptized unto Moses"*** meaning the Children of Israel were taught the Laws during the time of Moses after being delivered from the Egyptians. Likewise today the Children of Israel shall be baptized/taught the laws in the faith of Christ.

Water baptism symbolizes an Israelite cleansing their spirit (mind) from sin by prayer and by keeping the Commandments. In the same manner as the body must be washed physically from dirt with soap and water, so must the mind be cleansed from sin with spiritual water by the Laws. Our minds are dirty with sin, adultery, hatred, lying, homosexuality, drunkenness etc. only the Laws can cleanse those sins, not water. The Israelites no longer have to be baptized in water as **John the Baptist** practiced, but must now be baptized with the commandments in the faith of Christ.

 Matthew 3:11: *" I indeed baptize you with water unto repentance: but he that cometh after me is mightier than I, whose shoes I am not worthy to bear: he shall baptize you with the Holy Ghost, and with fire."*

John the Baptist did cleanse the Israelites from sin, by baptizing them in *"water."* This act was symbolic since he was only preparing the way for **Christ by teaching Israel to repent,** whose baptism would be with the *"Holy Ghost and fire,"* which was fulfilled in **Acts 1:8** and **Acts 2:38.**

 St. John 3:30: *"He must increase, but I must decrease."* The ministry of **Christ** concerning repentance had to *"increase,"* whereas **John**'s ministry of water baptism had to *"decrease."*

157

St. John 4:1 " When therefore the Lord knew how the Pharisees had heard that Jesus made and baptized more disciples than John."

St. John 4:2 " (Though Jesus himself baptized not, but his disciples)

This scripture clearly shows that Christ himself did not conduct water baptism but taught the scriptures that Israel may repent in His name.

St. John 15:3: " *Now ye are clean through the word which I have spoken unto you.*" **Christ** taught that the baptism that made Israel "*clean*" was the keeping of the Commandments, which he had "*spoken*" to them.

St. John 17:17: "*Sanctify them through thy truth: thy word is truth.*" To "*sanctify*" means to cleanse from sin. The truth can be explained in Psalms 119:142.

Romans 6:3-4: "*Know ye not, that so many of us as were baptized into Jesus Christ were baptized into his death?*

Verse 4, *Therefore we are buried with him by baptism into death: that like as Christ was raised up from the dead by the glory of the Father, even so we also should walk in newness of life.*" The "*baptism*" of **Christ** is putting the old man to "*death,*" and then raising up the new man in Him,

Ephesians 4:23: *And be renewed in the spirit of your mind;*

Ephesians 4:24 " *And that ye put on the new man, which after God is created in righteousness and true holiness*"

This is how we ought to "walk in newness of life," as the keeper of the commandments and true worshippers in Christ.

Acts 3:19: *"Repent ye therefore, and be converted, that your sins may be blotted out, when the times of refreshing shall come from the presence of the Lord."*

The Children of Israel must *"repent"* from their sins and be *"converted"* by applying the Laws in their daily lives, and not by being baptized with water. This is how their *"sins may be blotted out"* by the **Most High**.

Ezekiel 18:30: *" Therefore I will judge you, O house of Israel every one according to his ways, saith the Lord God. Repent, and turn yourselves from all your transgressions; so iniquity shall not be your ruin."*

Finally, being baptized with water does not wash away the *"transgressions"* which are sins such as: adultery, theft, fornication and homosexuality, etc. Therefore, the Most High will *"judge"* every Israelite who refuses to *"repent"* from their sins, by keeping the Laws through **Jesus Christ.**

SHALOM.

The Valley of Dry Bones

- **Ezekiel 37:1:** The hand of the LORD was upon me, and carried me out in the spirit of the LORD, and set me down in the midst of **the valley which was full of bones,**

  2: And caused me to pass by them round about: and, behold, there were very many in the open valley; and, **lo, they were very dry.**

  7: So I prophesied as I was commanded: and as I prophesied, there was a noise, and behold a shaking, and the bones came together, bone to his bone.

  8: And when I beheld, lo, the sinews and the flesh came up upon them, and the skin covered them above: **but there was no breath in them.**

  11: Then he said unto me, Son of man, **these bones are the whole house of Israel:**

160

<u>Why were the Israelites compared to a valley of dry bones?</u>

Proverbs 21:16 "The man that wandereth out of the way of understanding shall remain in the congregation of the dead."

Baruch 3:4 "O Lord Almighty, thou God of Israel, hear now the prayers of **the dead Israelites,** and of their children, which have sinned before thee, and not hearkened unto the voice of thee their God: for the which cause these plagues cleave unto us."

Our people are dead today because they have wandered out of the understanding that they are the Israelites, and suffer for breaking YHWH's laws. As Blacks and Negroes they wander in false man made religions as: Catholics, Baptists, Jehovah witnesses, Seventh day Adventist's, Muslims, and Rastafarians. This also includes non denominational religions.

But then the bones came together and flesh formed and they stood upon their feet. This means many of our people are waking up to the prophetic truth that they are the Israelites. They are learning their National origin, but their was still **no breath**. No Repentance!
Here is the breath that gives life:

Genesis 2:7: And the LORD God formed man of the dust of the ground, **and breathed into his nostrils the breath of life;** and man became a living soul.

Proverbs 7:2: Keep my **commandments, and live;** and my law as the apple of thine eye.

John 11:25: "Jesus said unto her, I am the resurrection, **and the life: he that believeth in me, though he were dead, yet shall he live**

Keeping the Commandments in Christ gives us life.

Revelation 14:12: Here is the patience of the saints: **here are they that keep the commandments of God, and the faith of Jesus."**

"This makes it clear that as repentant Israelites we must keep the commandments and the faith in Christ.

So although some know they are Israelites there is no breath in them. They refuse to either keep YHWH's laws or reject Christ as Messiah! Just knowing you are an Israelite will NOT get you eternal life.

I Corinthians 13:*2:* "And though I have **the gift of prophecy**, and **understand all mysteries**, and **all knowledge**; and though I have all faith, so that I could remove mountains, **and have not charity, I am nothing.**"

I Timothy 1:5 "Now <u>the end of the commandment is charity</u> out of a pure heart, and of a good conscience, and of faith unfeigned:"

This explains that the end (fulfilling) of keeping the commandments you must also have the fruits of the spirit.

Galatians 5:*22:* "But the fruit of the Spirit is love, **joy**, peace, longsuffering, gentleness, goodness, faith, *23:* Meekness, temperance: **against such there is no law.**"- no condemnation. Remember we suffered YHWH's curses because we did not have JOY in keeping his laws.

Deuteronomy 28:47 "Because thou servedst not the LORD thy God with <u>joyfulness, and with gladness of heart,</u> for the abundance of all things; 48: Therefore shalt thou serve thine enemies....."

There are many Israelites standing and walking without breath. There are congregations with leaders and members that are filled with hatred, jealousy, strife and contention etc.

Galatians 5:19: Now the works of the flesh are manifest, which are these; Adultery, fornication, uncleanness, lasciviousness,

20: Idolatry, witchcraft, **hatred, variance, emulations, wrath, strife,** seditions, heresies,

21: Envying, murders, drunkenness, revellings, and such like: of the which I tell you before, as I have also told you in time past, that <u>they which do such things shall not inherit the kingdom of God."</u>

3 John verse 9: "I wrote unto the church: but **Diotrephes, who loveth to have the preeminence among them,** receiveth us not.

10: Wherefore, if I come, I will remember his deeds which he doeth, **prating against us with malicious words:** and not content therewith, neither doth he himself receive the brethren, and forbiddeth them that would, and casteth them out of the church.

11: Beloved, **follow not that which is evil,** but that which is good. He that doeth good is of God: but he that doeth evil hath not seen God."

So just as **Diotrephes was, so are many Israelites today.** Unless they repent they will not inherit the Kingdom.

SHALOM

Come out of her

- *Revelation 18:4:* And I heard another voice from heaven, saying, **Come out of her, my people, that ye be not partakers of her sins, and that ye receive not of her plagues.**

- This verse proves the Israelites are captive in America/Babylon the great. We must separate from America's Politics, Religions, and all other Philosophies to not partake in their sins and keep the commandments in Christ to be accepted by YHWH. Then we will not receive of the coming plagues which is: sickness or disease, terrorist attacks, natural disasters, and biological warfare.

Deliverance

- **Jeremiah 16:14** Therefore, behold, the days come, saith the LORD, that it shall no more be said, The LORD liveth, that brought up the children of Israel out of the land of Egypt; *15:* But, The LORD liveth, that brought up <u>the children of Israel from the land of the north</u>, and from all the lands whither he had driven them: and I will bring them again into their land that I gave unto their fathers.

- The deliverance from <u>**NORTH** America</u> will be greater than the deliverance from Egypt.

Isaiah 8:20

- "To <u>the law and to the testimony</u>: if they speak not according to this <u>word</u>, it is because there is no light in them."

- Meaning if your ministers are not teaching you the Laws and testimonies of the Israelites, it's because there is no truth in them.

Shalom/Peace

Bibliography

- **Cover Model: Melissa Young**
- Russian Icons by Father Vladimir Ivanov
- The Library of great masters Michelangelo published by Scala/Riverside
- The Borgias by Marion Johnson published by Holt,Rinehart,Winston.
- Christ Paintings by Nathanyel Ben Israel
- The Voronet by verlag fur fremdsprachige Literaur
- Harpers Bible Dictionary published by HarperSanfrancisco
- The World of the Bible book 3 published by Educational Heritage,inc. 1964
- The World of the Bible book 1 published by Educational Heritage, inc. 1964
- History of Slavery by Susan Everette
- **Great Grand Parents Charlie Beckwith Sr. & Eppi Adams, Holly springs, N.C.1905**
- Blacks in Antiquities by Frank M. Snowden,Jr.
- Great Ages of Man Ancient Egypt by Lionel Casson and Time Life Books
- Pictorial History of the slave trade by Isabelle Aguet
- Picture History of Jewish Civilization by Harry N. Abrams inc.,Publishers
- The Israelites by Time Life books
- Seeds of change by Viola and Margolis
- Haiti feeding the Spirit photo by Les Stone

Printed in the United States*
By Bookmasters